BY DOG SLED FOR BYRD

DEDICATED
To
MOTHER
And
MARGARET

John S. O'Brien—Surveyor for the Byrd Antarctic Expedition

BY DOG SLED
FOR BYRD

1600 MILES ACROSS
ANTARCTIC ICE

By

JOHN S. O'BRIEN

ILLUSTRATIONS BY
RICHARD RODGERS
AND BEN STAHL

THOMAS S. ROCKWELL COMPANY
CHICAGO 1931

A PATHFINDER BOOK REPRINT EDITION
Complete and Unabridged

Printed in the United States of America

ISBN: 979-8-8691-3525-4

T HIS long dog team journey was a rare combination of hardship, danger, romance, adventure, and science.

It cannot help but appeal to the young people.

To Dr. Gould, the party leader, and his aides, Crockett, Goodale, O'Brien, Thorne, and Vaughan, the Antarctic Expedition owes an enduring debt of gratitude for the scientific results achieved.

The rest of us who did not get a chance to make this journey envied them, for it was the essence of adventure.

R. E. BYRD,
REAR ADMIRAL, U. S. N., RET.

CONTENTS

LIST OF ILLUSTRATIONS

YONDER the far horizon lies,
  And there by night and day
The old ships draw to port again,
  And the young ships sail away.
And go I must, and come I may,
  And if you ask me why,
You'll find my answer in the stars
  And the white road in the sky.

—GERALD GOULD.

Chapter I

SOUTHWARD BOUND

LEADEN, overcast skies hold the promise of an on-coming blizzard. An icy wind, sweeping in from the Ross Sea that lies far to the northwest, brings a raw, biting cold that sears one's face like a keen-edged blade, and stings fingers to the bone when gloves are removed for a moment.

In the strange, grayish half-light that envelops the endless expanse of snow and ice, ghostlike figures move about. Strange figures, oddly shaped and clumsy in their loose-fitting polar clothing. They remind one of a company of bears walking erect. Now one dives into a tunnel entrance, gopher-like, to emerge in a few minutes with a pack sack or a pair of skis and hurry along to a row of five sledges. These stand directly in front of the dog kennels, on the western edge of the settlement.

Here and there stand groups of three or four fur-clad men in earnest conversation, now scanning the sullen sky with anxious looks, now calling out to those passing to and fro between huts and sledges. Except for the ever-increasing moan of rising winds, a strange quiet prevails. Yet tension is high. For this is just twenty minutes after one on the afternoon of Sunday, November 4, 1929, and within the next few minutes one of the most remarkable journeys on record will begin. The geological party that forms part of Admiral Byrd's South Polar Expedition is preparing to drive across the icy wastes of that treacherous barrier that has snuffed out the lives of many brave men who have tried to wrest its secrets from their snowbound stronghold.

We, who comprise the party, know full well the dangers, hard work and possible suffering that lie before us. What our rewards may be we dare only hope. Many times we have lived over in thought that terrible journey of Captain Scott and his brave men, dragging on and on through the blinding blizzards and withering antarctic cold, only to perish within a few miles of the base that held food and life for them. Often have we discussed Sir Ernest Shackleton, another gallant Englishman. His attempts to reach the Pole were always beset by unfortunate and unavoidable incidents that would have discouraged a weaker man. After fighting through almost superhuman obstacles, living for days on short rations and making forced marches, he was obliged to turn back when within ninety miles of his goal. And we know, too, that the great Norwegian, Amundsen, and his party were called upon to the utmost of their endurance in being the first to reach the South Pole.

Is it any wonder, therefore, that we are all just a bit tight-lipped this morning, and that the rest of the camp also realize that maybe they are to shake hands with their pals for the last time? For over a year we forty-two men have lived together; together we have built our base camp, Little America, on the small bay of Ver-sur-Mer that was part of the Bay of Whales. Here, near the northern edge of the great Ross Barrier, we have been doing the slow, hard preparatory work that must precede any trip out into the Antarctic wastes. During the long months when the thermometer dropped to an average of fifty-one degrees below zero, and for weeks on end, when we lived in the deep gray darkness of a winter below the Antarctic Circle, our little group had grown to know each other as only men can who are cut off from all the rest of the world. And so, whenever a party sets forth, anxiety is hidden under the cheery good wishes of those who remain behind.

The time is drawing near now, the time for which we have been preparing so many months. See the dogs! Even they sense the unusual. Another time they would be jumping frantically to the length of their chains. Now, down beyond the little group of huts, they sit on top of their kennels, row on row, like soldiers at attention. Not a sound do they make, but with ears alertly cocked, and shining eyes, they follow every move. Once we are ready and take our leaders to their places, the lid of an inferno will be off and the huskies will make the barrier echo with their excited howling. Now, they wait for the signal.

Admiral Byrd and Larry Gould, the latter the geologist who is to lead our party, are pacing back and forth, the Admiral giving Larry some last minute instructions. Huddled in their furs, they both look heavy, though Larry is really broader in build. Mike Thorne, our lithe, athletic ski expert, takes a last look at the slim runners he is to use and which are now lashed under his sledge until he gets under way. Freddie Crockett, whose tall, slender build gives no hint of his great reserve strength, has his face half-hidden behind a pair of green goggles as he brings out a radio generator and makes it fast on his load. Goodale, working with that quiet dependability that always engenders confidence, is beside me as we give our equipment a final inspection before bringing out our dogs. We have learned that it is best never to harness the animals until we are ready to go, so great is their excitement and desire to get under way.

The zero hour has come. There goes Norman Vaughan after his leader, Dinty. And that is a signal for the rest. Instantly all the huskies break into such a chorus of barking and howling that one can scarcely make himself heard without shouting. Now we all start leading out our teams, one by one. Rather, I should say, they lead us out to their place in the gang line, for it is all one man can do to hold these fellows by the collar.

Dinty, with his handsome black pelt and white face

and feet, his great plume of a tail waving joyously, stands in front of the inseparables, Moody and Watch, with three more pairs to complete their team. My own brown and white Labrador huskie, Pete, looks anxiously at me from his position at the head of my team. Pete has a funny little way of looking round, with a questioning tilt to his head whenever he doesn't quite understand an order, or when he can't see why he is being held back from starting. So, one by one, the teams are made ready.

Each of the sledges has a stout rope fast to the rear end, which in turn is tied in a slip-knot to a stake driven deep into the snow. This prevents the team from starting before we are ready. It takes stout ropes and deeply driven stakes to hold the anxious dogs from dashing off helter-skelter today. As the animals are brought to their places and harnessed, a group of willing volunteers has to help hold them in place. We work fast now. The dogs are all harnessed. Larry is shaking hands with the Admiral, who now comes to each of us to bid us good-bye. "Good luck, boys," he says. "Come back safe."

We hastily grasp the hands of all our friends, each of them wishing us a heartfelt Godspeed. Then we take our places at the gee-pole of our sledges. Larry, who drives no team of his own, climbs on Vaughan's load. He turns and grins at us. "All set?" he asks. We wave our assent. "Then let's go!" The anchor ropes are jerked loose, the men holding the dogs leap back.

No command is needed, for with one jump the dogs are away, snow flying in clouds from their racing feet. We are off at last on the long, cold trek. Vaughan is in the lead, looking like a mammoth butter ball as the air swells out the loose gray-white windproof that covers his woolen parka. Larry turns to give one final wave, loses his balance, and rolls off into the snow. But he is on his feet in an instant, the dogs are held back, and amid shouts of laughter that break the solemn sadness of a moment ago, we are off again.

Our hands are full now. Clinging to the sledge and guiding a dog team that is running at top speed demands all a man's attention. The surface is bumpy, and care must be used at all times if we are not to be upset. The dogs gradually settle down to a more steady lope as we leave Ver-sur-Mer and head southward across the uneven ice of the Bay of Whales.

Once upon the bay we are confronted by Antarctic's most dreaded weapon—blizzard. This is serious because the treacherous, ever-changing bay ice has undergone enormous changes in the last twenty-four hours. Towering pressure ridges—those huge, jagged elevations of ice formed by the shifting currents—have been thrown across the former trail over this area.

Larry realizes at once that we would be wasting valuable time chopping out our old trails that had been mapped so carefully in advance for this very journey. Dangerous as it is, hunting new routes with open water on every hand, and unable to see ten feet ahead, he resolutely swings westward toward the very center of the bay. With long open leads of water on all sides, half-blinded by the flying snow, swerving, skidding, dodging, we swing along at a racing speed.

The dogs respond to our shouts of "gee" and "haw," but their animal sense of danger is far keener than our ability to direct them. Time and again, of their own accord they swerve sharply aside with breath-taking suddenness, escaping by a few inches some huge crack in the ice through which the oily sea water is lapping hungrily for us. Without their instinctive knowledge of danger we might have steered directly into those cracks.

On and on we go. We have twenty miles to make this first day, and Gould is determined to push ahead regardless of blizzard or any other unlooked-for handicap. On and over and around we go, until at last, after six miles, we swing back once more to our old trail, with a mile still to travel before we reach the barrier, that great mass of ice that for centuries has kept men from penetrating to the heart of the Antarctic. But a few have made the crossing, and we know it can be done.

One immense pressure ridge stands directly across our path. These great snow-crowned, glittering ice ridges are not necessarily dangerous if enough time is allowed to inspect them and lay out a trail before they are crossed. Formed as they are, by the action of the sea causing the ice to buckle and heave up sometimes as high as fifty or sixty feet, broken and jagged, men must go in with shovels and ice picks, leveling, bridging, and filling, until a semblance of a trail sufficient for a sledge is made. But even with these precautions it is a thrilling adventure to cross a big pressure ridge, for once the dogs are under way they never stop. They tear through, upsetting sledges, spilling drivers, never halting unless snagged.

And so we swing along, headed for our last hurdle. Vaughan, with Larry aboard, is in the lead, the rest of us trailing in single file. And now all the drivers except Vaughan grasp the lashes of their sledges and dig their heels into the snow to break the speed of their teams and allow greater distance between units. This is a precaution against a pile-up in the pressure. Although a road has been cut through for us some days ago, it is narrow and rough.

Swinging sharply to the left, Dinty takes the slight slope approaching the ridge on the dead run. Up they go and are soon lost from sight behind a big icy shoulder. In about two minutes we see them emerge on the other side, pulling up on the smoother surface of the barrier. One by one we each race through the pressure, and one by one we come out without mishap, drawing up beside our leader on the barrier. Seven miles of rough going are behind us but we still have thirteen miles to travel before calling it a day. We stop a few minutes to give our dogs breathing time and to readjust and tighten our loads, which have taken considerable beating across the ice. Luckily for us, there had been no serious accidents, and so no breakage.

Adjusting a harness here, making a lashing fast there, we then dress for riding. On go sturdy windproof trousers and, as extra precaution, dry mukluks are donned. Woolen parkas are removed, and we pull fur ones over our heads. These knee-length coats have fur hoods attached. The hood has a projecting edge of fur which protects the face from the wind; that is, except when the wind is coming directly toward the wearer's face. The parka fits snugly and is usually worn with a flap that goes between the legs and buttons up in front, thus keeping the garment held close to the body and defying icy winds that try to creep under one's clothing, bearing chill in with them. The fur, with a tough fabric called "windproof" over it, is wonderful for keeping out wind without adding much weight. Big fur gloves, loose and warm, are donned. The clothing we take off is made fast to our sledges, so placed that air and sun will dry any moisture. We have learned that clothing must be changed whenever we make a stop, for our exertions cause perspiration, and one of the greatest foes we have to fight is dampness. In this climate moisture will freeze easily, and we are running no needless risks of chill and frostbite. Once our clothing is changed we sit down for a smoke in the lee of the sledges.

A supporting party has preceded us for two hundred miles, laying out trail. Every half mile they have stuck a bamboo reed that has an orange-colored flag attached. Experiment has shown that orange is the only color that can be seen for any distance on the barrier. Black or red are worthless because of the shadows formed by the rolling character of the surface. Only the orange stands out against white snow and also against dark shadows. But blizzard is another matter. And although the storm has abated somewhat, the wind still holds, and the fine, granular barrier snow is swirling about in eddies like a sand storm. The sun is still hidden, and the visibility is therefore decidedly bad.

"Those flags are going to be tough to pick up," observes Larry, taking a deep drag at his cigarette. "Better stick close together. Norm and I will lead off, but all hands keep a sharp lookout. There are some bad crevasses about three miles south according to the supporting party's report." A few more puffs and we are off again.

It doesn't take Norm long to get Dinty straightened out, and soon we settle down to that steady, mile-eating trot that is the most efficient gait for sledging.

It is difficult to describe what it is like—traveling when sky and snow blend. There is no outline, no horizon, nothing definite by which to judge distance. The team just ahead seems to be miles away; it is so out of proportion. Mike Thorne once gave the best explanation of what it is like, when he said, "It's just as though we were driving in a bucket of milk." The flags appear suddenly, seeming to spring out of the snow only a few feet from us. It means constant watchfulness, and, because of our dark snow glasses, is a considerable strain on our eyes. We at last remove our glasses in order to sight the flags more quickly. The sun is hidden and so we think we are safe from getting snow blindness. While—glasses off—we are able to pick out our trail marks with greater ease, yet we are to pay dearly for this folly within the next few days.

It's cold business, this riding. Despite furs and windproofs, the frigid breath of the barrier creeps upon us. Feet and hands begin to feel the chill after a short period of inactivity. To combat the cold a driver must jump off and run alongside the sledge, a trying job when visibility is poor. Hummocks and depressions in the surface cannot always be seen. But we must keep warm; so we each grab our gee-pole and stumble along as best we can until we are in a glow, then drop back on the sledge for a rest. In a few minutes we get up and do it all over again before our perspiring bodies become chilled. There is no easy, comfortable way to sledge the icy wastes. It's all work —hard, grueling work.

And so the miles slip by on this first day out. The temperature is about ten degrees below zero, which is about right for good sliding. The wind is dying down now; the snow has stopped drifting; the horizon becomes more distinct, the white of the barrier contrasting vividly with the blue-black sky. Still the dogs jog along, while we are now riding, now trotting along beside the sledges. We are traveling about a quarter of a mile apart. It is very quiet—the silence of a dead land—silence undisturbed for thousands of years. Nor is this the silence of a temperate zone. Here are no trees to rustle in the wind; no soft patter of tiny animal footsteps; no insect life to make little humming sounds. Life? Since we have turned inland from the coast, all life has been left behind. A few stray gulls are all we will see, besides our own party, that live and move.

A tiny dark spot appears directly ahead, perhaps three miles away, the marking flag of our first emergency food base, twenty miles from Little America, laid down by our supporting party. Shortly the snow wall that has been built about the little tent containing the stores becomes visible. The dogs see it; they speed up a little. They, too, realize that ahead are food and rest. Now they break into a dead run, barking, snapping at each other to discourage loafing. Vaughan, first in, passes the cache and then swings sharply to the left, driving off the trail about a hundred yards before stopping. One by one the other teams follow, coming to a halt directly behind each other in a row back of the first sledge. It is just seven o'clock. We have covered twenty miles in about five and a half hours, and feel well satisfied with the first day's trek.

The dogs drop down, tongues dripping, sides heaving, tired, but happy that their day's work is over.

CHAPTER II

IN CAMP

WHILE the rest start changing their clothes, Goodale and I quickly unlash the cook tent and carry it to the smoothest part of the barrier, about fifty feet from the sledge train. In a few movements it is spread flat. The corners are pegged down, back to the wind. One goes inside with the seven-foot pole; this is inserted through the top, with the base resting upon a flat board provided for that purpose in order to prevent it from settling. That finished, the corner guy-ropes are stretched and pegged down into the hard snow. It has taken less than two minutes to get the cook tent up.

Next, from another sledge, we bring the primus stove,

the food box, two kettles, and the thermos bottle. In less than five minutes we have made the cooking gear ready for Larry, who is to take care of the inner man. Now Goodale and I are free to follow the example of the others and don our warm, dry clothes. Even though we have ridden our sledges considerably, the running we did between times has caused moisture to form and freeze; so we need to change.

First, off with the damp mukluks, or reindeer skin boots. On go warm, fur-lined socks, over which are pulled the huge canvas boots that our sailmaker, Martin Ronne, has made for us. These boots are half-filled with senna-grass, a growth found in the Arctic, looking very much like hay and valuable for absorbing moisture. Next, the windproof trousers are replaced with long fur ones. Then a warm, dry woolen parka with windproof over it; we have been wearing our fur parkas while riding, and woolens form a very comfortable substitute. Now we get on dry gloves and are ready to care for our dogs.

Attached to each sledge on either side are rolled two long strands of aviation control wire, perhaps three-eighths of an inch in thickness, very strong and flexible. These we stretch out at right angles, and make the loose ends secure by driving a three-foot iron rod through a loop on the end of each wire and pegging it deep into the snow. The wires are each about fifteen feet in length, and spaced along them are dog chains. These are a foot long, soldered securely to the wire with a strong snap on each chain. These are our picket lines, arranged so that the dogs cannot get close enough to each other to fight. They also prevent the animals from uprooting the picket line, as the loaded sledge in the center acts as an anchor.

This picketing of the dogs is one of the most important problems confronting men on the trail. The dogs must at all times be secure—not only because they fight to the death if they gain their freedom; but also because they will eat not only food, but harness and lashings as well. Many expeditions have been seriously crippled because the dogs got loose and went on a rampage of maiming each other in wild fights, and then topping off the performance with a light lunch of lashes and harness.

The lines out, we now put the dogs "to bed." Each team is treated in the same fashion. First comes the wheel pair, the first two next to the sledge. The lead lines, those short lengths fastened to the main gang line and attached to each collar to keep the dogs in file, are unsnapped, the belly band is freed, and the whole light harness is slipped over the animal's head. Each in his turn is taken to his place on the picket line. The dogs that are driven on the right side, go to the right side of the sledge; the others to the left. The harnesses are then picked up, starting from the sledge, and each is hung on the gee-pole beside the collar of the dog to which the particular harness belongs. This orderly method will save time when next we harness up. Everything is now shipshape.

Feeding comes next. The animals sit quietly at their places, alert and patient while we are arranging the harnesses. But when we start to open the canvas tanks containing the food, they get busy scolding us to hurry. Whines, barks, and half-suppressed growls indicate their state of mind. They have worked hard and have waited long enough! Each driver takes out enough pound-and-a-half cakes of pemmican for his team. Now they really do get noisy as they see that at last dinner is about to be served. They jump and bark and beg, each straining at the end of his chain.

We haven't the heart to tease them, and throw each his ration as quickly as we can. They grab it between forepaws, crouching and chewing hungrily, growling at their neighbors all the while a warning to "keep off." A few finish sooner than the rest and stretch to the length of their chains to get at the next fellow's meal. A warning snarl and a lightning snap, and the intruder quickly minds his own business and decides that his own ration is all there is coming to him.

One by one they give their chops a few licks, nose around for any crumbs of food they might have left, and then do their regular two or three turns before lying down on the cold, hard snow for a well-earned rest. These huskies can sleep comfortably in the cold and snow. Their long outer fur forms a protection that sheds water and keeps moisture from penetrating to the thick, wooly under coat. And so they sleep calmly under a light downfall of snow, secure in the knowledge that a few turns and shakes will rid them of the clinging dampness when they get up again.

All this time Larry has been getting supper. As he

is not quite ready, we employ the waiting time in making camp. We have tried to arrange our loads as efficiently as possible, so that the things we need first are loaded last. Norm, Fred, and Eddie use one tent; Mike, Larry, and myself the other. We pick out a smooth spot on either side and in alignment with the cook tent. Our sleeping tents are the type called "*A*" tents, and are orange-colored two-thirds of the way down, so that they may be easily visible if we wander a short distance from camp. The two poles sewed inside the cloth in both front and back are lashed at the top and spread out like a fan at the bottom to the width of the floor, or about seven feet. These poles are sharp on the ends.

A man stands at the front; another at the back. First, the front and back poles on the left side are jammed into the snow, with the sewed-in canvas floor pulled taut. Then the front and back poles on the right side are similarly handled. The front and back guy-lines are stretched and secured, then the three guys on either side are stacked, and our house is up and ready for occupancy.

But we still have one more job before we can leave the tent. At the bottom of each, and on the outside, a piece of cloth about a foot in width has been sewed on all four sides. This is called an apron, and upon this apron we shovel snow, piling it up two or three feet. This assures the stability of the tent by preventing wind from getting under the floor, and also forms a wall as protection from blizzard.

The entrance to our tent is not the usual turn-back

flap used in temperate climates. Such a flap would let in cold and wind. Our entrance is a circular hole, about two feet above ground, and just large enough to admit the body of a heavily-clothed man. Around the edge of this hole is sewed a funnel of canvas about three feet long. Antarctic etiquette demands that when anyone enters a tent he pull this funnel in after him and tie it like the neck of a bag, to shut out the wind and cold.

The Admiral will want word from us tonight; so Freddie Crockett must get his radio rigged. The antenna poles, bamboo in two fifteen-foot sections, are joined and set up about a hundred feet apart, held in place by long guys. This antenna is placed behind our row of tents, with leads coming off the aerial through small holes in the back of the tent, to be attached to the set. The radio gear is brought in from Crockett's sledge, and he promptly gets busy hooking it up. The rest of us haul out our sleeping bags, and after arranging our fiber mats on the floors of the tents, lay our bags out and flop down on them for a little rest and a smoke before supper.

We can hear the dull roar of the primus stove in the cook tent. All of us are ravenous and not much given to conversation. We want "hoosh." Gee, Larry is slow. At last, as we wonder how much longer we must be patient, there it is—the long awaited call. From out of the cook tent comes a loud, high pitched yell: "Mike— Norm—Fred—Eddie—Obie— come and get it!" He never had to call twice in all the time we were on the trail. In we would climb, pulling the door skirt inside to keep out the wind. Supper was always the best meal.

*There were seven miles of travel like this before we crossed the treacherous and ever-changing
Bay ice and reached the Barrier proper*

(*Above*) First of all the radio must be rigged, for the
Admiral will want to hear from us

(*Below*) Each man has his duties in making camp, and no
time is lost in waiting for one of the units of the party

Not only were we able to satisfy a tremendous appetite through plenty of good food, but it was the period of relaxation. Breakfast always found us cold and hurried, but no matter how difficult the day had been, no matter how tired we were, we always relaxed at supper. Conversation that had been pent up during the solitary marches was released, and topics ranging from the details of the job at hand to events and incidents of home life were gone over again as though we were once more living those moments.

Our table manners are a bit unique, for in the cook tent we are very crowded for space. Each has to balance his food between his knees, for we have no table, nor could we find space for one. The tent has a perpendicular side wall that reaches just to a man's head when he is seated. The roof rises higher at the center and at the top is a hole about four inches in diameter. This is to let the cooking steam out. If we did not have it, condensation would make the interior damp and uncomfortable.

In one corner sits Cook and Food-Dispenser Gould. Before him is the square food box into which, each night, we place the bags of food allowance for the next day. This box, together with the stove, is always lashed on top of his sledge, so that we can get at it quickly at meal time, without having to unpack other gear to reach for it. On one side of Larry is the primus stove. On his other side are gray canvas bags that contain food. He looks like a judge behind the bar, only he is going to dish out grub instead of sentences. First we get a drink of melted snow, for we always are thirsty at the end of a long pull—and sometimes quite a while before the end, for that matter. Lying on the food box is our first course, brown Eskimo biscuits, larger than a graham cracker and much thicker. These are buttered, and upon each lie three crisp pieces of bacon. Although very tasty and satisfying, one must have good strong teeth to get the best of these biscuits.

When we finish that course, the cook places six tin mugs on the top of the food box. Each has its owner's name scratched on the side. Now comes "hoosh," a mixture of soup and the heavy, filling pemmican. This latter is a mixture of meat and fats, squeezed dry and cut into cakes about four inches square and an inch thick. Two more biscuits are served with this, but it is a little easier now, as we can resort to that rather indelicate process known as "dunking." One must protect his teeth a bit, for these biscuits are granite-hard.

It takes two heaping mugs of "hoosh" to even dent our appetites, and then there is a big argument as to who gets the kettle it was cooked in to clean up. Larry settles this by designating a night to each of us for this added bit of ration. Then comes either tea or cocoa, and sometimes a half square of sweet chocolate is added for dessert. This, with cigarettes, completes the meal.

Our conversation is varied on this, our first night. Much anxiety is expressed regarding the dogs. A few are not in the best of condition; Lady has left her small pups behind and is missing them; some of our dogs are very young and we are speculating on their ability to stand the rough going they will receive. But Norm believes in the youngsters. "I don't care if those four dogs are only six to eight months old," he expostulates, "they have been thoroughbreds today, and you'll see they keep the pace."

Norm is right. All four are to prove their worth, and we are to have a lot of sport with those youngsters: Cocoa, Sky, Al Smith and Kit Carson, this last named after an older friend whom the Admiral visited in the Philippines when he was a lad of twelve.

Then we talk of our equipment, and some changes are suggested for various parts. Minor changes these are, having more to do with the handling while on the trail, for we are convinced that our gear is the best that is available and most suitable for our purposes.

Mike Thorne has had no part in the conversation for some time but has been sitting quietly with a far-away look in his eyes. At last Larry turns to him with, "What are you thinking about, Mike?"

With rather a sheepish grin Mike replies, "Do you know, fellows, I spent the better part of three days making a very careful list of every bit of personal equipment I carry in my pack sack, jotting it down in a notebook. Thought it would be a big help in locating my gear. And now I have come away and forgot the book!"

The ceremony of washing dishes is dispensed with from now on, and with our wooden spoons we have cleaned them fairly well and stacked them in a corner. Larry boils another kettle of water and adds a half pound of oatmeal to this, leaving it on the fire for just a minute or two after it boils. He takes it off, and out of a canvas bag dumps in a small handful of raisins. The oatmeal he pours into a thermos jug and shuts the top, letting it stand on the food box. By morning this will be cooked to a delicate brown, and with the raisins forms a delicious breakfast.

This use of oatmeal is an innovation in sledge trip food. The folks back at camp were a bit skeptical about it, but Larry tested it out before starting, and the food was so easily prepared, takes so little space and has such light weight for its bulk, that it certainly proves itself an addition worth having. With so little variety possible, this hot cereal each morning became one of our most relished foods. And it certainly is wonderful for fighting off the chill of the early morning. Once Larry has the oatmeal in its container there is nothing more to do now but get ready for bed.

And so we all duck our heads and crawl out through the cook tent door, tying it up securely behind us. The dogs have had a good hour's sleep and some of them are getting up, stretching and changing their positions. So we go over and play with them a little while. They bark a greeting and pull on the end of their chains to get near us. Each day of our long journey, when the work has not been too exhausting, we follow this custom of an evening romp with the dogs. Odd, how friendly and gentle these big animals are with us, while with half a chance they would be fighting savagely and bitterly with each other.

Frederick Crockett goes to his tent and starts tapping out on his radio the WFAT that forms the call letters of Little America. Soon he establishes contact and we report our first day's progress and hear in return that all is well at the base camp. We all wait for this news. That finished, we crawl into our sleeping bags, first removing all of our clothing except the heavy woolen top shirts that we wear. Half buried in our bags each man makes entries in his diary. But this is a pretty cold job, writing a few lines, then putting our hands in the caribou fur bag as fingers get stiff from handling a pencil in this temperature. None of us keeps an elaborate record for this reason. Notes and references give us enough data. We finish this work quickly, and with much moaning and struggling each man snuggles down further into his bag, pulling the shoulder flaps closely around his neck.

Despite the fact that our mattress is the hard, cold snow, it is a marvelously comfortable bed, and very restful. The narrow mat that each man lays beneath his bag is made of thin slats of fiber and can be rolled into a small packet when not in use, but when spread out gives just enough air space between the bag and tent floor to keep the warmth of his body from melting the snow beneath. Again that precaution against moisture, for therein lies our great danger. Dry cold we can face, but get any part of the body damp and then have to expose it for a split-second to the cold, and the moisture freezes and makes the cold unbearable.

Thus we settle down for our first night on that journey

for which we have been planning and working all through the past months of dark antarctic winter. It is very quiet here. Sometimes a growl or smothered bark from one of the dogs; again, the loud cannon-like boom of cracking ice as a small crevasse is formed; or the wind singing in our guy lines. Larry, Mike and I in one tent, and the "Three Musketeers": Norm, Fred and Eddie, in the other. We six are at last on the trail over the great Ross Barrier ice fields, a trail that is to take us within three hundred miles of the South Pole. Success or failure depends not only on us but also on those careful preparations that have made this journey possible and that really formed adventures in themselves.

CHAPTER III

BACK-TREKKING

ADMIRAL BYRD'S Antarctic Exposition started for the polar regions in August, 1928, with more than one objective. He not only hoped to fly over the South Pole and determine the sort of country to be found in the southernmost part of the world. He wanted to explore as much territory as possible and perhaps find new lands to add to the map of the world; to take aerial photographs, so that all findings might be accurately recorded; and to make scientific studies of the country. The physics, radio conditions, meteorology, geology, and a half dozen other scientific investigations were to be undertaken.

That was where we came in. It was the study of land

formation that our party was to pursue. Laurence Gould, our leader, was a geologist and geographer; George Thorne—commonly known as "Mike"—was a surveyor, as I was, also; Crockett was our radio man, and we all, except Larry, had to help Vaughan and Goodale with the care of the dogs, as well as drive our own teams. Larry had elected himself to the job of cook, and nobody ever envied him in all the time we were together.

A glance at the maps of the north and south polar regions shows at once how much more is known of the Arctic than of the Antarctic. Here, before us, was work that meant high adventure. There were more or less authentic rumors of coal and other mineral formations of which other explorers had found trace in the mountainous regions nearer the Pole. There were mountains off in that hazy southeast that man had never seen. Perhaps we might find lichens or primitive animal forms to prove that animal and vegetable life had existed in these regions before the great ice-cap descended upon it. Even the kind of stone that composed the mountains would tell a geologist a story of what this land was like in ages gone by.

Here was opportunity to "put things on the map" in no slang sense of that phrase. Is it any wonder that we were anxious to face hardship in order to seek the land that lay beyond the barrier ice, and adventure into the unknown?

Just before the summer of 1928-29 ended, Gould, Balchen, and June took the Fokker plane to the Rockefeller Mountains, a hundred and fifty miles east of

Little America, on a surveying trip. A terrific blizzard caught them while in camp and destroyed the plane. They had a pretty serious time of it until aid reached them, but as Kipling would say, "That is another story." Still, the loss of the plane cut down our ambitious program for field work this second summer. The Ford tri-motor plane had to be kept for aerial photography and the polar flight, and, although Admiral Byrd offered us every consideration and aid possible, it was necessary for us to face the fact that if we were to go to the mountains to do our work we must go by dog team. This involved a tremendous amount of preparatory work.

Through the dark days of winter and the graying light of spring we worked out detail after detail with the utmost care. Who could tell what seemingly small defect could bring failure? Improper food for his dogs had hampered Scott's first expedition; neglect to carry a life-line nearly cost the life of a member of the Borchgrevink party, who fell into a crevasse headfirst; scurvy attacked more than one expedition because of lack of balanced diet. Wherefore we planned with utmost care.

First we had to select the dogs. Through fights and disability, the number of available dogs for the trail had been cut to the minimum. Of those that remained, some were not in the best of condition and some were young and inexperienced. And so all during the winter we concentrated on building up the dogs, carefully nursing those that had been wounded in battles, administering tonics, and constantly watching them, in order to prevent fights that would result in more casualties. Some of the puppies, born on the barrier, had to be trained, but the four youngsters we took with us certainly proved themselves to be worthy of their breed.

Next was the dog food, or pemmican. This is a concentrated food, different from pemmican for humans, containing among other things cod liver oil, chopped meat, and meal. It has a tremendous food value and will serve the same purpose as nearly twice the weight in fresh meat under hard working conditions. It came to us in bags of about sixty to seventy-five pounds apiece. We saw that if we were to take these bags on the trail and each day chop off the dogs' meal there would be considerable loss in splinters and chips and a great deal more loss in time. To overcome this, nearly three weeks were spent in molding this food into one-and-one-half pound cakes, which was the weight arrived at as sufficient for a dog's daily meal.

The pemmican was brought into the mess hall, warmed until it became the consistency of bread dough, placed in wooden molds that had been cut to the right size, and then set outside to freeze. Although many disagreeable hours were spent over this sticky mess, and we were the butt of considerable joshing for our unappetizing cookery, we were more than repaid for our trouble when out on the trail.

Dog harness was another vital factor in assuring good transportation. More than one piece of harness had to be replaced by new gear, and old pieces were reinforced at the points that had shown weakness during our sledging operations so far. Added care had to be taken that they fit the dogs perfectly. A dog harness improperly made or badly fitted soon causes sores and consequent lack of efficiency. The Alaskan gang hitch was used.

Next came the sledges. The double-ended freight sledges that we were to use were quite heavy, so Bernt Balchen and Sverre Strom built us new and lighter ones. When they had finished, we had three beautifully-made twelve-foot freight sledges, weighing about half as much as those we had brought out to Little America with us. The workmanship of these two men was wonderful, and a good share of the credit for the success of this trip is due to their excellent products.

We used three smaller, single-headed Norwegian army sledges as trailers, each unit being composed of two sledges. Two of us used the sledges we had brought down with us, and to offset the extra weight of these we cut down a little on the loads they carried.

On these sledges we lashed canvas tanks which had been measured and carefully made to fit by Martin Ronne, who could tailor anything from clothing to tents. Each tank was about eighteen inches high and extended the full length of the sledge. It had overlapping flaps on top and after we had stored our supplies and equipment into a tank, the flaps were carefully closed. Around this we ran our lashings from one side of the sledge over the load and back, making a very compact load. Man and dog food was kept in the tanks, while tents, pack sacks, fuel and stoves were lashed on the outside. Crockett had his radio lashed on top of his pack, so he could get it up as soon as we settled each day.

This idea of using tanks on the sledges was not new with us. Amundsen had used them and considered them far more convenient than lashing a number of odd-shaped bundles to a sledge, as Scott had preferred to do. There was really less danger of things working loose when small articles were fastened in a tank, especially when a sledge tried to investigate the interior of a crevasse, which was not an unusual occurrence.

Next we considered the man food. Its quality we knew to be of the best. Dr. Coman, physician for the expedition, had chosen all the food we took to the Antarctic. He had estimated the daily food needs for a man. It wasn't enough to have a person *feel* well fed; he must *be* well fed. Foods that gave body heat and strength, as well as foods that protected from disease, he rationed out. For instance, the raisins in our oatmeal tasted good, but we would not have given space to carrying them if they had not also had definite food value. The lemon powder in our tea was an insurance against scurvy, that disease which has attacked so many polar parties. No detail was too small to consider in choosing food that must maintain strength at its best, and yet add as little weight as possible on the sledges.

Our job was to pack the food so that at all times it would be protected from the weather, yet easily accessible. And so, day after day during the long Antarctic night we sorted biscuits, soup rolls, pemmican, malted milk tablets, chocolate, tea, and other items of food. We sorted them, weighed them, counted them, and put each day's rations in an individual bag. When we camped, we simply had to pull this bag out and there was a day's food; three meals for six men.

This food for the day was kept in the food box lashed on the outside of the sledge, and each night the next day's rations went into the food box when we camped out.

Fuel containers were another vital problem. Lose your fuel when traveling on the barrier and chances of pulling through are very much against you. To Tom Mulroy and Victor Czegka goes the credit for finally perfecting a reinforced gasoline tank of five gallons, and another of one gallon capacity that served us very well all the time we were away. Czegka also made the gasoline-burning primus stove that we used for cooking and for melting all our drinking water.

Then came clothing. We had studied a great deal about the clothing necessities for the Antarctic and had brought down with us a wide variety of the best clothing possible. However, what was suitable for one did not work out for the other, and so we were constantly experimenting with various kinds of gloves, with types of footwear, with combinations of woolens and wind-proofs, until our original stock was entirely overhauled and altered to suit each particular case. Here is a list of the exact items of clothing we took with us. There was no hit-and-miss, but each man checked his typed list that had been made in duplicate to cover equipment for man and dogs. My list read:

1 fur parka	2 pairs of mukluks
1 fur pants	1 pair ski boots
1 woolen parka	1 pair canvas boots
1 woolen pants	2 pair caribou socks

1 large windproof parka	1 pair moccasins
2 windproof pants	8 pair woolen socks
1 windproof shirt	2 pair heavy oversocks
2 woolen shirts	1 pair felt liners
2 suits heavy underwear	2 pair felt inner soles
1 sweater	1 pair fur mittens with liners
1 fur hat	2 pair canvas mittens with liners
1 woolen helmet	2 pair extra liners
1 scarf	2 pair windproof cuffs
	1 pair woolen wristlets

The extra amount of footgear was needed because they would have hard wear and also, because sore feet or frozen feet might put an end to the whole expedition. We had found that the felt inner soles could have a few holes punched in them without lessening their heat-giving qualities, and that this made them keep dry longer than if there had not been these tiny air spaces in them. Even such a small detail as this was carefully studied and tested before our equipment was finally chosen. If care and study could avoid a single discomfort or mishap, we gladly gave time to find the very best thing to do or use on our hazardous journey.

As we were to travel most of the distance on skis, another item of clothing had to be studied; our ski boots. We had brought with us the Amundsen type of boot, specially made for use in the coldest weather. Most of us fellows found these too big and cumbersome, especially for summer use; so they had been cut and adjusted to our liking. Mike Thorne made Larry and himself a pair of boots much smaller, yet large enough for sufficient socks, and these worked out very well for them.

On the coldest days we might wear three or four pairs

of socks, a pair of felt liners and a handful of senna-grass inside our boots. Not only were the socks themselves warm, but the layer of warm air that formed between the layers of material gave added heat to help fight off the cold that worked its way even through all that amount of covering if we stood still for any length of time. So, naturally, our ski boots had to be large for winter wear. But this was a summer expedition, and we were content with a couple of pairs of socks and felt liners, together with a layer of senna-grass to take up any perspiration. Boots made for the winter were too large, and we couldn't risk the irritation that comes from shoes in which the feet rub around. Still, neither could we allow them to fit closely enough to impede circulation. So it is easily understood that having our footgear fit properly was a serious consideration.

Our sleeping bags, fur side in, had the entrance made a distance from the top, with windproof flaps to pull around one's neck, or over the face when sleeping in the open. We were warned to use the flaps for face covering and never to breathe into the bag lest dampness result. The windproof was thick enough to keep in the warm breath and thus help warm the sleeper's face in bitter weather.

Charts had to be made, maps drawn, record books prepared. Instruments such as theodolites, thermometers, a pocket compass for each man in addition to the ship's compass lashed to the leading sledge, and barometers, had to be checked, tested and packed. The rate on watches was taken all winter by Larry because we must have the correct time when making solar observations. Larry's office used to resemble a pawn shop with all those watches hanging around, on which he was keeping a record.

Nothing was left to guesswork that could be planned ahead. The route to be followed and the work to be done were outlined in a preliminary report. Every item was listed. We knew how many ounces of food a man needed for a day's rations and what foods it should contain. The same was true of the dog food. We planned on ninety days in the field, marking in advance how far we could travel each day, but making liberal allowance for a certain amount of delay. When we had counted out everything we would need, from food and clothing to extra dog whips and pocket knives, every item was weighed, so that we knew to a pound just what we would carry. This was necessary because the dogs had just so much pulling strength, and we didn't propose to waste one bit of it. Every item that could be cut out was discarded but nothing was left behind that might help us on the trail. Thus we even gave space to a few books because we knew they would be needed if we were held up by storm and fog for days—as we were—and while we waited about for the polar flight. An onion skin paper edition of Shakespeare, a few technical books, Hudson's *Green Mansions,* and H. G. Wells' short stories were among the few books taken with us.

Thus we were occupied during the months of darkness from April 18 to August 24, while the thermometer

Bernt Balchen and Sverre Strom spent many long hours constructing the light and efficient sledges which helped so much in making the trip a success

Packy was one of the pups born on the Barrier, and I brought him back with me

We would give the dogs a brief rest before entering a bad piece of pressure ice.

hovered between fifty and seventy degrees below zero. Finally, when the light came back to us, we started training the dogs and ourselves as carefully and thoroughly as a vaudeville team would train. The dogs, pent up in underground snow tunnels all winter, were almost unmanageable. They were so full of life and energy that they fairly ran away with us when brought out to be driven for the first time. We would start them in easy, letting them run for a short distance with light sledges for the first three or four days, gradually increasing distance and loads as their condition warranted. This not only perfected the dogs' condition, but our own as well. It made us more efficient in the handling of skis, and accustomed the dogs to answering commands promptly.

Soon the time drew near when we were to start. Our function in the field was two-fold. First, to survey Queen Maud Range, study the glacial flow, and collect geological data; second, to stand by in readiness in the event of a forced landing during one of the airplane flights. Our base near the mountains would be marked with a cross of orange flags to indicate a safe landing place. We were to travel to the south about three hundred and ninety miles. When all necessary equipment was assembled, we found that our loads were tremendously heavy, averaging between one thousand and twelve hundred pounds.

In order to save time and also to provide us with more supplies than our dogs could haul, a supporting party of three units, comprised of Walden, Bursey, De Ganahl, and Braathen, with Walden in charge, was sent out in advance. They preceded us south for two hundred miles, establishing food depots every fifty miles for our use on the return trip. They also marked the trail for that distance. By this arrangement we could proceed much faster, while they had to take the time to navigate by compass. With the orange colored flags that they set down each half mile as trail markers, or even closer in bad areas, we did not have to bother with the compass, but simply followed along their trail. Yet even that did not prove as simple as it sounds, for blizzards frequently made visibility a matter of inches, and we groped along, half-blinded. Or, as we found in the first few miles out, the ice had shifted over the pathway and forced us to make a new trail. The route laid down by the supporting party took us over the barrier ice for about two hundred miles. From there on we would have to do our own navigating for nearly another two hundred miles of snow and ice.

It was about ten days or two weeks before our final departure that the supporting party left. One man went ahead on skis to guide the teams, set a straight course, and look for crevasses. Sometimes he was roped to the next man when the going was very bad. Vaughan, Crockett, Thorne, Goodale and I accompanied them for the first hundred miles, taking with us more than half our loads.

We had to get an early start, and the temperature was very low, but it was a great opportunity to work out our gear and make any corrections that might be necessary.

We completed this trip in eight days and cached our supplies at the end of that distance, ready to be picked up when our expedition reached that point. This extra trip hardened the dogs to trail work, and the lighter loads we would have to carry when we started on the long trek made longer daily pulls possible from the first. Otherwise there would have been terribly heavy loads to haul during the first part of our expedition. For that matter, the dogs probably thought they had pretty heavy hauling, as it was!

Back in the base camp, we gave the dogs and ourselves about five days' rest and then started out again on the final trip, Larry in command this time. All this tremendous amount of work and planning was necessary if the expedition was to succeed. It is by anticipating every conceivable possibility that one can win through. The slightest error in judgment may prove costly, even fatal. Away from their base, the men are entirely "on their own," and it is then that the advance work helps or hinders progress.

No wonder our entire supplies and equipment weighed almost 5,400 pounds, exclusive of what we had taken out in advance. Besides the food, shelter and clothing, we needed over ninety pounds of meteorological, navigation and surveying instruments; eighty-three pounds of equipment for both motion and still cameras; three hundred pounds of radio gear; dog gear, exclusive of over a ton and a quarter of dog food, was fifty-eight pounds. Tools, trail markers, safety devices, and sledge equipment added two hundred and fifty-five pounds more.

We had made typewritten lists of everything and then studied them for weeks, trying out various substitutes to lighten our loads where possible. Each man checked his personal list to be sure he had every item necessary and then checked again against his actual supply. Every new idea was tried out; so when we actually got away, we were carrying only the most necessary supplies. Even so, the total weight was formidable.

When, at the end of the first hundred miles, our trailers were picked up, the loads were divided to carry about eight hundred pounds on the forward sledge and three hundred on the trailer. This division made for safety in crossing fragile snow-bridges over the crevasses.

Effort was made to foresee every possible contingency, prepare for every emergency. Yet who could tell? What lay ahead of us in those icy wastes?

CHAPTER IV

TRAVELING LIGHT

MORNING—cold and overcast and quiet—only the low moan of the wind and an occasional rattle of chain as one of the dogs moves about. It certainly is fine inside the sleeping bag! Larry, who sleeps between Mike and me, is up. Well, we have about twenty minutes more before breakfast. Now you can hear the dull roar of the primus stove again, such a comfortable, soothing sound on a cold morning. And then, just as we are about to doze off, again comes the old war-cry: "Mike, Norm, Fred, Eddie, Obie, come and get it!"

We would like to have breakfast in bed, but servants are hard to get on the barrier, and we know Larry is very temperamental in that matter. What is more, he sure can get us up. All of the past winter that was part of his job, getting the whole camp out to breakfast, and though the fellows nicknamed him "Simon Legree," after the most picturesque slave-driver in literature, they surely did get up. What's more, they all approved of "Uncle Simon," as they gradually began to call him. So, with a final stretch, we heave ourselves upright. Oh boy, but this surely is the coldest time of the day! We put on the heaviest and warmest clothes that we have and one by one we drop into the cook tent. Breakfast, at best, is not always a cheery meal. Down here it is not served under the best conditions. No chairs, no table, no linen, no morning newspaper, or fresh fruit. We crouch on the canvas floor that overlays the ice of the barrier and are a rather quiet gang as we wait for the oatmeal. Piping hot it is, with thick milk, made by adding water to a powdered milk preparation. The raisins give it a wonderful flavor, and after two mugs of this and a big cup of hot tea we begin to feel better.

If we are to cover our twenty miles today there is no time to be wasted. As soon as breakfast is over we start breaking camp, while Larry prepares the "ob" to carry along for our noon meal. This word "ob" was coined in Little America during the time we were making our camp, and the originator of the term is William "Cyclone" Haines, our official meteorologist. Whenever the snow-shoveling got heavy or the hands got a little bit cold, Bill would cast his eye up at the sky and remark to his assistant, Harrison, that they had better take an "ob," meaning that they would take a balloon observation for wind direction, which necessitated relieving them from hard manual labor. Many times an observation scarcely seemed necessary, but who were we to question these great scientists in their work? Off they would go, and then, after a little while we might find Bill and Harry in the mess tent taking an "ob" over a hot cup of coffee and a sandwich. The term soon became general and all noon meals were "obs."

And so Larry was now preparing our noon "ob." That consists of tea in the thermos jug, squares of pemmican to be cut up and eaten raw, Eskimo biscuits and chocolate. While he is doing this the rest of us are busy breaking camp. The dogs by this time are jumping around, barking and displaying that never-failing energy these wonderful animals have.

First comes the radio. The antenna poles are lowered and disjointed, the aerial wound on a spool, and the generator box and other equipment brought over to one of the sledges. Then down come the tents, rolled and lashed; sleeping bags are thrown on top of the loads and secured, sometimes fastened down, but often lashed so the wind will get into and dry them.

By this time Larry has finished his preparations, and the thermos jug is placed in a specially-made box to keep it from shaking about and being damaged. The bag containing the noon meal is lashed beside it. Now the cook tent is down and the primus stove and food box are placed on the sledge. All this time we are working in heavy clothing and are gradually warming up. As we are to ride for one hundred miles before we take to our skis, we are wearing the same clothes throughout the day at present, though gloves are changed frequently, to avoid frostbite.

And now we harness. The gang line is stretched out ahead of the sledges and we bring our leader to his place. One by one the dogs are put into their proper positions. The picket lines are rolled and tied on front of the sledges and we are ready to move. Although it does not seem that this operation should take much time, we are never able to get away in less than an hour from the time we get up. We work quickly but never dare risk carelessness in the smallest detail.

The first mile out of camp every morning is always very exciting. The dogs are so eager that they are beyond control and the minute we shout at them—and often we do not even get a chance to do this—they are away in a bunch. This usually means that we have to stop two or three times, separate them from fights, untangle their harness, and generally straighten them out. After that first dash they calm down and get squared away.

We have found it most efficient to drive the teams in single file, leaving about three hundred or four hundred yards of distance between each team and the next in line. Running them alongside each other we find tempts them to fight and race. That sort of thing, of course, expends their strength uselessly and puts an unnecessary drain on their reserve power. Believe me, we are not wasting any of our supplies unnecessarily this trip, least of all our supply of dog-power!

And now starts the same old routine of monotonous, lonely riding and running. We ride until we begin to feel stiff, then jump off and run beside our sledges until warmed up again. This single file travel is certainly lonely. All day long, day after day, we have no chance to talk except when we get together at "ob," and then we are hurried. Only dogs and a few gulls add life to the white landscape, and soon we will pass beyond the region frequented by gulls. The penguins were left behind the first day out.

The sky is still dark and overcast, and while the temperature is about five degrees above zero there is a strong southwest wind blowing that makes us ride with our backs to it. The wind is what makes it unbearable, but fortunately the temperature is never very low when the wind is strong. Otherwise it would be impossible for a human being to stand the weather.

Mile after mile we make, shifting our position on the sledge for comfort, beating our bodies with our arms to keep warm. We pass the hours away in speculation as to what lies before us after passing that first hundred miles we have traversed before. About a hundred and fifty-five miles from Little America we know that what is called the "crevassed area" must be crossed. The supporting party has reported back that it was an extremely difficult and dangerous sector, and that they had had some mighty narrow escapes while crossing the thinly-bridged, bottomless chasms. They have warned us that the greatest care will be required in order to get our heavy loads across these fragile bridges. And so the monotony is lessened by planning the best method of procedure when we arrive at this dangerous area, and these plans are discussed at length when all six of us are gathered together at mealtime.

Driving continues each day until about noon, and then Larry calls a halt. Vaughan draws his team a short way off the road and the rest of the sledges are run in and ranged alongside each other, the dogs resting in their traces, usually too tired to want to "start anything."

Then off comes the food from the top of the load and our chilly "ob" is eaten, washed down by hot tea. From one-half to three-quarters of an hour is usually consumed in this manner, with conversation and a couple of cigar-ettes serving as dessert. Tents are never unlashed at noon. We get in the lee of one of the high-piled sledges if the wind is strong, but on a quiet day the open ice-plain is our dining room. The last possible puff extracted from a cigarette, and then the sledges are swung back into the trail and are off for the long afternoon journey.

Our average distance is about sixteen miles a day now. This is done deliberately in order to work the dogs into the best of shape. They must not be spent and worn when we reach our extra loads. At about half past four or five o'clock we begin to look for a camping ground again. This found, the sledges are swung into camping formation and the one-night stand is built over again.

Supper and talks of home and of the trail ahead, plans for the future, a short and hasty radio talk with our base camp, and usually a romp with the dogs end our day. Then come the hurried entries in diaries, and good-night.

Despite the fact that we are in the midst of the summer day that lasts for months and gives us only a pearly gray twilight for a short time instead of the dark night that we were used to in America, we manage to sleep soundly. All the fresh air, coupled with hard work, seems to do the trick for us, and there is precious little insomnia on this journey.

In the morning again come those dreaded moments waiting for Larry's breakfast call, the hurry to break camp and get away. But one duty was never neglected. Each morning the sleeping bags were pumped full of fresh air. Catching them up, with the entrance hole wide open, the upper side was alternately lifted and dropped until fresh air had been forced to the very bottoms, so that any moisture that had come from the heat of our bodies was air-dried. Every third morning the bags were turned inside out about a half of the way down and each hung on its owner's sledge in a way to catch the wind and give an even more thorough drying down to the very bottom.

One thing didn't take time, and that was washing. Not only did our clothing go unwashed, but we ourselves dared not use water on our skin. Just try a couple of months without a good washing, not even to mention a bath! A few feeble attempts were made to wash our hands, but the danger of having the water turn to ice and give us frozen fingers was too great to be worth the risk. Larry, although he was cook, did little better than the rest of us. Safety first! Washing was a really dangerous proceeding in this atmosphere, for our tents were cold places at the best. Therefore, even he could not live up to sanitary regulations. A dry rub was the best he could do except when, later in the journey, some of the dogs had to be sacrificed and used as food for the others. Then he did run the risk of a real hand wash. Besides, hot water meant using fuel and as we had to carry every drop of gasoline we could not risk running short.

Shaving also was dispensed with and a lot of assorted colors in beards soon decorated us. Crockett came out with a red beard, but most of us were content with more sober colors. One thing we did was brush our teeth each day, since sore gums might prove as serious as sore feet. Just the same, is it any wonder that, as we followed the same dull routine of driving and running, our dreams of luxury were of *real* food, hot baths, shaves, and clean sheets, as well as clothing that had water instead of air for its cleansing?

It was on our second day out, after a breakfast of hot oatmeal and tea that we saw the supporting party coming toward us, back from their trip of two hundred miles to lay down supplies for us. We stopped for a chat with them, getting extra information about dangerous areas ahead, and then, after a sociable cup of chocolate malted milk, watched them trekking for home while we faced the unknown country to the south. I think it was Freddy who complained that traffic was getting heavy in the Antarctic, "Running into all those men today, and next there will be planes passing overhead. Getting too blamed crowded down here for my taste!" Well, he wasn't to suffer from crowds for some time to come.

It was the next day that we learned a lesson that we didn't forget in a hurry. We traveled twenty-two miles and advanced but two. And this is how it happened. The visibility was awful but we were so sure of picking up the flags that we failed to watch the big compass. Goodale led off and none of us paid much attention to the way we were going. After a time it seemed to us that we had gone quite a distance without seeing a flag, but the dogs were in a fighting and snarling mood that day and in straightening them out we quite lost any sense of direction. After a time we finally saw a flag waving in the distance and made for it, only to find we were back in the camp from which we had started that morning!

We figured we had simply circled the camp; so, after a bit of grouching and razzing, we started merrily on our way again. Nobody noticed that we had come back into camp from the south and were continuing in the same direction we had come. The afternoon before we had passed our abandoned snowmobile that had been left in the snows where it had broken down some weeks previously. And now, after a couple of hours' travel, suddenly out of the mist loomed a tall beacon. "Looks like the snowmobile," Vaughan suggested. "But how on earth could that be?"

"My heavens, are we headed north!" Larry cried. "Stop those dogs and let's see where we are." All the sledges drew up and out we tumbled to investigate, and there was that snowmobile where we had left it the day before, and we had circled round back to it. Now, too late, out came the compasses, to find we had put in a lot of energy traveling backward! Well, what we said was more emphatic than polite, and it didn't take us long to get going in the right direction. But we advanced only two miles beyond where we had camped the previous night and never again did we trust to our sense of direction without the aid of a compass in a land where there was no definite horizon line or landmark to guide us when the sun was hidden.

<h2 style="text-align:center">Chapter V</h2>

<h2 style="text-align:center">DOG DAYS</h2>

WISH those dogs could hand over some of their early morning pep to us. They've got too much and we could do with a little extra," one of the fellows remarked as we hitched up on a blustery morning. Our fingers fairly froze inside our gloves, the wind stung our faces, and it was all we could do to keep from being grouchy. Oh, for another hour or two of sleep in our warm sleeping bags!

But those animals! They certainly were the world's champion dogs. They had shaken off the covering of snow that had been whirled on them by the wind during the night and were ready to start. Most of them had taken a few bites of snow, which is a husky's idea of a drink. In fact, some of the pups that had never been out of the Antarctic had to be taught to lap water. They didn't know what to do with the stuff!

During the day the crack of the whip in the air above their heads was usually enough to set them going right. But we never could cure them of that mad start each morning that tangled them into a fighting mass, and often we had to bring the whip down hard to save some dog from worse punishment by his mates. Such a snarling, biting mass of fur and fangs as they were!

Once straightened out, they went to work with a steady pull. It was as if they said, "Well, we've had our morning sport. Now let's get to work."

The young dogs were awfully funny at times. The pep displayed by our four youngsters was remarkable, and often-times quite irritating to the older fellows. When we stopped for meals these young chaps insisted on barking and jumping around, and starting the teams by themselves, seemingly never tiring.

Cocoa, so named because his coat was all red-brown, and his brother, Sky, black and brown, had been allowed to run loose so much in Little America that they couldn't understand this business of being tied up all the time, and were constantly yelping and complaining about it. They didn't take to harness as readily as eight months old Al Smith did. Al certainly won his spurs. Born on the barrier, as were the other youngsters, he had had to get out and battle his way ever since he had been able to walk. A perfect type, brown and black, plume tail, ears sharp and alert, he took this trip as a lark.

No matter how long the march was, the youngsters never seemed to tire. They were an excellent argument against the theory that a dog younger than a year old will not stand up under hard sledging conditions. And no matter how much disturbance they caused, they never bothered big, patient Turnavick who was picketed next to these pups. When they got tired barking, they spent their time chewing the ears of this beautiful gray and black veteran, but he seemed to make allowance for their youth and sat patiently, eyes half-closed, and let them maul him to their hearts' content.

Blizzard, leader of Goodale's team, was a one-man dog. Typical gray husky, he allowed anyone to pet him but showed no enthusiasm for anybody but Ed. Yet let his master come near and he was begging for attention, and would stand on his hind legs with his forepaws on the man's shoulders, looking straight into his eyes.

In Norm's team we had a pretty little mother dog named Lady. Some time in her life she had been mistreated and for that reason was very timid. We all made a business of showing her we were her friends, and she grew to trust us, though she was always shy when strangers were near. During the past winter, when it was sixty below zero, she brought six beautiful little huskies into the world. No human mother could have showered more love and attention on her children than Lady did on her four boy and two girl babies. The pups were born in the snow tunnels where the dogs were wintered, and I never knew where I would find those pups. I used to heat milk and take it down to them. Lady would always meet me at the entrance and proudly lead me to one of the kennels she had lately taken possession of. The next day she would lead me to another apartment perhaps in another tunnel. Lady always moved them, one by one, into the kennel of one of the big male dogs, much to the chosen one's delight. I sometimes think she was raising those babies to be traveling salesmen.

When we left for the trail, it was hard to take Lady from her babies. She was not in the best of condition, either, and her black coat was rather ragged. She was thin and whimpered a lot and was terribly lonesome for her pups. She was paired with an old fellow who grew annoyed with her whimpering and barking. He stood her nervous, temperamental behavior just so long, but nearly every day, usually at noon, before Lady quieted down to take a little rest, the old fellow would reach over and take a little nip to quiet her. Then he would get remorseful and nearly pull her right to him, as much as to say, "I am sorry that I lost my temper with you, you poor thing."

But, with all her whimpering, Lady was a thorough-bred, pulling as hard as any other dog in the camp. She pulled all the way to the mountains, but at last she dropped, and although we lashed her on a sledge and let her rest and ride, she was too far gone, and we had to lose her in the end.

My leader, Pete, was a fine dog. Not as heavy as some of the others, he pulled well and was a perfect leader, seeming to smell danger when he couldn't see it in fog and mist. When he would come and lay his head on my knee and look up into my eyes, I could feel the love and faith he could not put into words.

Then there were the Siberian twins, Oomiyak and Kayak, so identical that it took me weeks before I could tell them apart. Oomiyak is the word for a double passenger boat, and kayak for a single boat. Black, with markings of dark brown on face and chest, every mark seemed the same on the two dogs. They were the gentlest, most lovable dogs of the entire pack, and faithful hard workers. They had none of the boisterous, rowdy playfulness of the others. And affectionate! When I would bend over to take one of them from the picket line to harness him, the other would put a paw gently against my knee as if to say, "I don't want to disturb you, but how about a little petting?" Of all the dogs in my team I loved them best, for they had characters many a human being might envy.

Behind these two were harnessed Bus and Frosty. Bus was a good worker and friendly, but snow-white Eskimo Frosty was a bully. He would snarl all during lunch hour and all evening before he went to sleep, but he was the biggest bluff that ever lived. It didn't take Bus long to find this out and he would wave his big plume tail calmly and settle down without paying the least attention to all his running mate's threats. But Frosty was a deliberate trouble-maker. His snarling would make the other dogs peevish and nervous and soon there would be two or three fights going. But Master Frosty was never mixed in any of these rows. Trust him to keep out of any fighting! All he wanted was to get the other dogs started and then sit innocently to one side watching the excitement.

The wheel team next to my sledge was the snow white Dingo and his running mate, jet black Targish. Biggest and strongest in the pack, they had the most remarkable strength I have ever seen. From the moment the harness was arranged on them in the morning, preparatory to getting under way, until they were put on the picket line at night, regardless of how heavy the day had been, they never stopped barking and straining to be away. On more than one occasion those two started off by themselves to pull the entire load of a thousand or twelve hundred pounds on my sledges. They couldn't be left alone with the load for a minute or they would be off on a tear, trying to make their way to the South Pole before morning. And bark! They didn't seem able to run without making a noise about it. But no one minded that. It was rather comforting to have the dogs make a bit of noise to break the deadly stillness of those long days. Besides, this wasn't like the ugly, growling noise of Frosty, but just the joyous bark of dogs that were having great fun pulling the sledges along.

I remember one noon a fight started in Crockett's string of dogs. We had to leave our lunch and go over to quiet them. Finally we took out one of the offenders and replaced him with another dog. All this time their leader, Quimbo, lay at the head of the gang line with his nose on his paws, apparently paying no attention to the uproar. When we had completed the exchange of dogs and gone back to our lunch, Quimbo very quietly got up, walked back to where this new dog stood, and bit him on the neck. Not hard, just a little nip. Then he returned to his place at the head of the line and lay down again. It was as if he had said, "You are a newcomer in this team. Just you understand I am the leader and boss dog. Now don't you think you can start any funny business around here." What is more, the new dog evidently understood.

Quimbo was mostly black, with brown markings on his face. He was one of the largest dogs in the pack, and quite trustworthy. Although very friendly, he did not seek attention and was decidedly dignified in behavior.

But the twins that were stabled next to him, Dolph and Cito, never could get enough petting. They were simply tireless seekers for attention, but it must be said that they were equally tireless workers on the trail. These two gray and black beauties were marvelous. Long legged, big of chest and shoulder, fast and smart, they were really more of the racing type. Nevertheless, they proved themselves excellent pullers when called upon for regular, steady work.

Over on Mike Thorne's line could be found another pair of twins. They carried the sporting names of Firpo and Cy. Two more nondescript gentlemen have never been seen. They were more "just dog" than husky. But what dogs they were! These two were veterans of the trail and knew how to pull along the icy stretches. Very quiet and docile while on the picket line, once they were in harness they had a queer habit of starting a dog chorus between themselves that never let up. They seemed to try to out-voice one another by barking constantly into each other's face, and the faster they ran, the louder the din they raised. How they ever managed to have lung-power enough to keep the running pace and yet raise such a racket, was one of the things that puzzled all the men on the expedition, and we never found the answer to that puzzle.

Red and String came next in this group, two most efficient workmen. Tickle, leader of this string of Mike's, was coal black and one of the universal pets. He was a clever one, Tickle, forever trying to put something over on Mike, stealing anything he could get hold of, running away at the least chance, and forever cutting up, one way or another. But he was a great lead dog and as game as they come. He proved his courage and endurance later in the trip. When we were in the mountains he managed to tear the muscles on one shoulder, yet despite the pain and difficulty of walking, he hobbled all the long four hundred miles back to Little America on three legs. He may have been a scamp when he had a chance, but no dog on the expedition was friendlier, or a better leader, or showed more uncomplaining courage and wonderful endurance.

It would be almost too hard to pick out any dog and say he was the finest of all our strings. Every man had a secret love for his own dogs, and nearly every dog showed special devotion to his driver. Maybe the fact that each man fed his own dogs had something to do with that; at any rate, there was real affection between men and dogs. It was no wonder we loved them, for they showed such keen sense and often saved us serious spills in dangerous places. At the same time, like naughty children, they would get to racing and romping the moment our attention relaxed, and many a spill in the snow they gave us if we dozed while on the sledges.

Probably our star actor was Dinty, leader of Norm's team. He always demanded attention when any of us approached. He would sit on his haunches and fan the air with his paw as though a fly was annoying him, casting his head to one side the while. And he would keep this up until we went over to pet him. If we passed down the line without talking to Dinty or petting him, he was heart-broken. Other dogs were as beautiful as Dinty, with his black coat relieved by white stockings and a white blaze on his face. Other dogs were as affectionate, and clever, and hard-working. But probably no other dog combined all these qualities as did Dinty. The Admiral accurately described him as "a black Malemute with soulful eyes and the disposition of Puck."

More than once I was reminded of the good little boy in school, who always looks so innocent, yet manages to be at the bottom of most the mischief that goes on. That was Dinty, but you couldn't help loving him and laughing at his mischief even when it made extra trouble for you.

No doubt of it, Dinty was a bit of a joker, and smart as they made them. My first experience with him came a few days after our arrival in Little America. The camp was located about ten miles in on the barrier, and we had to sledge the freight from the steamers over the bay ice to camp. With the coming of spring and the resultant breaking up of the ice, it was decided to make the whole journey over the barrier. A trail had been picked out by the very capable Balchen and the teams went over it in safety. Still, there was no telling when the ice would break.

Every bit of building material, food, clothing, and equipment had to be unloaded on the ice and then carried by dog sledge from the ship to our camp at Ver-sur-Mer. And all this over ice that might change overnight. Several times the route had to be changed slightly to avoid new pressures or cracks in the ice. One morning our leader came to me with, "We are sending supplies over the new trail today. I'd like you to rope yourself to the leading sledge and precede it in order to test the strength of the ice. This is an extremely dangerous piece of business and you are at liberty to refuse if you choose."

After the awful monotony of waiting for the chance to leave shipboard, I welcomed an opportunity for some excitement, and was soon to have it.

Three teams were in the party, and soon we were ready to set off. I was in the lead, about fifty feet in advance, an alpine rope under my arms attaching me to the first sledge. As it happened, my previous education with sledge dogs had been sadly neglected. What I did not know about them or their habits would fill a good-sized volume. But I learned a thing or two that day! The normal speed of the sledge team when not overloaded is about a brisk trot that is maintained mile after mile with no let-up. Trying to keep ahead of these dogs in crusted snow that breaks under one's weight is quite a job. I did nobly for about two hundred yards and then thought a little rest was in order. But Dinty, who was leading the team, had other ideas on the subject. He felt that he hadn't even started to travel and that it was up to me to keep going, or else let someone point the way who knew how to do it.

Sweating and stumbling and swearing a bit, sliding and slipping along, I strove mightily to uphold the traditions of intrepid explorers, but I couldn't keep up the pace Dinty expected of me. And maybe that dog didn't know I couldn't! He just set out to make an embarassing situation into a hideous one. He would glide up beside me with that maddening, distance-eating stride of his, and just as he was at my side, over he would edge—oh, so easily, strike one of my legs with his body in such a way that it was thrown behind the other, and with a whirling spin, down I would sprawl full length.

Sometimes he would change his tactics and would deliberately run between my legs when I was in stride. And when I had landed with a thud and picked myself up again and regained the wind that had been knocked out of me, there would be Dinty, his team brought to a stop as he eyed me gravely as though to say, "If this is one of the guys who is going to explore for us, heaven help us!"

It was a humiliating situation, this being guyed by a husky. But good came of it, for if that barrier could stand the shocks of my meeting up with it that day, it proved itself safe for anything to cross on it. A two-ton truck could have passed over with safety. Besides, out of that experience, Dinty and I became good friends, after I had learned to keep going and not let one large-sized dog bowl me over. Now, a year later, on the trail, we had more than one romp together after I had visited with my own team at night.

It was always fun to watch Dinty when we patted his team mates, Moody and Watch. These two were great cronies. If we stopped on the trail, they would sit on their haunches and lean against each other. When stopping for lunch at noon one always laid his head over the other's shoulder. Beautiful dogs they were, big and powerful, with fine dispositions. Moody was all brown, with a majestic head like a lion, tireless in harness—an ideal sledge dog. When he put his paws on a man's shoulders, they were about the same height. He would look into one's eyes with a steady, friendly expression.

If you patted one of this pair, the other would nearly knock you down to get at you. It wasn't exactly jealousy, but they simply could not understand why they should be taken as individuals—what was Moody's was also Watch's. Try petting Moody, and big black and white Watch, with Dinty at his side, would nearly push you off your feet in their efforts to get their share of your attention. But if you persisted in petting one of the team mates, while the other still tried to "get in on it," Dinty would calmly settle beside the favored one and put one paw over his shoulder as though to say, "Well, it's all right with me if you like him best. He's a friend of mine, and I like him, too."

Yes, the dogs did fight, but they also had many notable friendships among themselves, and once affection was established between them, they seldom broke it for any cause. The old fellows would stand a lot of nonsense from the young ones and when they turned on them, did not inflict the severe punishment they would have given an older dog, except in extreme cases. And how those old dogs did delight in tiny puppies. They could lie for hours watching the babies crawl about, or keep perfectly still if the little ones sought warmth by curling up close to the big fellows.

From the time they were a few weeks old, the pups born on the barrier were trained to harness. Tiny sledges were made to fit their strength, and maybe they weren't the proud young things when they started out to haul a tiny load! Felt they were just as good as the big fellows then, and strutted and yipped and tried to run away with the load, just as their elders did. Sets of harness fitted to their size were made for them and care taken to have them fit comfortably. Nothing can more quickly ruin a dog than ill-fitting harness. It seems to make sores on their dispositions as well as on their bodies when harness chafes them.

On the trail we were constantly watching the dogs for signs of harness chafing or any indisposition. Special care was taken of their feet, although they were pretty good doctors themselves and licked carefully any cut or sore spot caused by sharp edges of ice that sometimes injured them. Fortunately their food agreed with them and their one meal a day sufficed to give them energy.

Men have tried all sorts of transportation on the barrier. Scott used ponies, and our expedition had a snowmobile, but nothing equals dogs as traction power on the ice. Only an airplane, soaring overhead, can compare with the dogs, and even that isn't a fair comparison, for while the plane can cover more territory and get aerial views, the dogs help the expedition do detail work. Our party quite shared Amundsen's belief that nothing would ever quite supplant dog-power in arctic and antarctic exploration.

CHAPTER VI

A HUNDRED MILES OUT

LITTLE AMERICA was five days behind when, on November 9th, we reached the cache that marked the end of our first hundred miles. There stood the loaded sledges we had brought on the advance trip in October. Our loads would be heavier now for a time with all that extra equipment to haul along. Each team would be hauling a thousand pounds, or half a ton.

Up to this point the trail was familiar. Beyond this cache stretched country that was new to all our party, although the first hundred miles of it had been marked by the advance expedition under Arthur Walden's lead. Nevertheless, here was where the real work was to start. So, for the rest of that day, it was decided to take things easy. We made camp and had a cup of tea. Our "ob" that day was light, probably because we were planning a large supper. George Tennant, the cook at Little America, had sent along with us three chickens prepared for fricasseeing for our Christmas dinner. Even that extra weight could not be carried now that we were going to pick up our heavy loads. Every extra pound had to be taken into consideration in order to help us reach our goal. Therefore, we decided to call the end of the first hundred miles a point for celebration.

Larry started the dinner as soon as we had camp arranged. He set some dried vegetables boiling and started cooking the chickens. The rest of us went ahead and fed the dogs. Then we rearranged sledge loads a bit and got everything shipshape for the next morning's early start. How we mourned the loss of the plane that, had it not been destroyed in a terrific wind-storm while on a geological expedition to the Rockefeller Mountains the previous season, could have carried us in hours where the dogs would take weeks to reach.

At about five o'clock the old clarion call was sounded from the cook tent: "Mike, Norm, Fred, Eddie, Obie, come and get it!" A couple of us nearly got trampled on in the rush. And what a meal! The dried vegetables when prepared properly are very good. The chicken, although cold-storage, had been boiled tender. Then we made a real feast of it by having some strawberry jam for dessert.

Gee, but it all tasted good after five days of "hoosh" and pemmican! And heaven only knew when we would get anything again that tasted like "real" food! That was the first time that any of us had eaten our Christmas dinner before Thanksgiving Day, but as Norm said, "We certainly got all the snow trimmings to make it *look* like Christmas, anyway."

There was more than plenty to eat, and we stuffed like small boys at a feast until we could hardly breathe. We finally got to bed at about half-past seven, and all of us had grand nightmares due to the change of diet. But for such cause we would have been willing to have nightmares every night!

And now real work was to start. On November 10, we set forth with our complete unit. At this time the program was changed a little bit because from this time on there would be no more riding. "It will be skiing from now on," Mike warned.

That was lots easier for him than for any of the others. He was an expert at the art while the rest classed as "dubs," with just a few months of experience. Still, there was nothing else to be done. The loads were heavy enough for the dogs without our added weight, and running along in heavy boots was out of the question. The thin, icy surface was beginning to break under our boots, leaving us stuck in the snows, at times knee deep. Even the weight of a dog was sometimes too much and a sledge would be slowed while one of the animals crawled out of a hole where he had been acting as an involuntary anchor. The farther inland we went and the warmer the summer sun became, the worse this condition would be. What we liked best was weather at about ten above zero, as that would melt the crust enough to make good sledding, but not soften the snows beneath.

When we broke camp and got ready to depart, just before leaving, our fur mukluks were removed and ski boots put on instead. Then skis were fastened on with heavy straps. The rest of our heavy clothing was kept on, just as before, because we were still somewhat chilled. However, after the usual straightening-out process on the first mile, we were well enough warmed to strip off some of our extra clothing. We had started out that day with alpine rope fastening us together at some fifty feet between each two men, and at first we had also roped the sledges. But soon we discarded the ropes between our loads. These had to be so near the ground that they were continually catching on hummocks or being snarled by the dogs when they raced or overturned their loads. We decided that part of a team would miss falling in a hole and be able to pull the remainder out, but we men had to keep roped until the more dangerous part of our journey was passed.

Sometimes our dressing room was the open Antarctic plain, or we might bend down behind the loaded sledges to cut off wind while making change of costume. Despite the warm sun it was bitterly cold. Doing one's dressing with the thermometer flirting around the under side of zero, and with snow and ice for a floor, has certain disadvantages.

In skiing with the dogs, sometimes we used the ski poles, and sometimes kept pace by holding on to the gee-pole which is attached to the front of the sledge. The preferred method depends entirely on the speed that the dogs are making.

When the temperature gets very low it affects the snow in such a way that a friction is set up between the surface of the snow and the sledge runners. That makes the sliding very hard work. It is as though the runners were dragging through sand. We experienced this difficulty during the first day we picked up our freight sledges. The thermometer registered between fifteen and twenty degrees below zero, a sharp wind was blowing, and the best distance we could make that day was twelve miles.

We did what we could to spare the dogs on their first day of heavy pulling, stopping for a minute or two in each second or third mile. The dogs would drop down in their tracks to rest, while we men would get together for a hurried conference, or huddle on our sledges. We would have been tempted to stretch out a bit, despite cold and wind, if it had not been for the long skis that were strapped to our shoes. It was hard enough to keep our feet in them. Every little while one of us would strike a bump in the surface and land in a huddle after a wild flight through the air!

At noon we were dripping with perspiration. The minute we stopped, off came our gloves, shirts and wind-proofs, and quickly we pulled on heavy sweaters, fur parkas and dry gloves. One of the features of the windproof material was that no matter how damp it became, hanging it out for ten to fifteen minutes would air-dry it perfectly. By simply rubbing between the hands, any frost remaining was removed.

After a hurried lunch we started out again. As we grew warm from our exertions, the process of taking off our heavy clothing was repeated. At night, before any of us did a thing, we always removed the damp gear again. This time even our ski boots and heavy socks came off, to be replaced with "fur liners," and then we were all set to go to work making camp in warmth and comfort.

This night we all feel a bit "down." Even the dogs share the feeling. Spy, the old veteran, snaps peevishly at Lady. Then, ashamed of his display of temper, he moves closer, puts his paw over her shoulder and begins to lick her face. Only Watch and Moody refuse to be disturbed, and sleep comfortably with their heads close together.

After all, what is the good of being an explorer? Why leave home and comfort for months of trekking over snowy wastes, perhaps never to return? Why sleep in stuffy little tents and have nothing but pemmican and hard biscuits and tea, when back home there are luscious steaks and coffee with real cream and— But in a few minutes, with the despised pemmican before us and the hot tea warming our chilled, weary bodies, we are ready to go ahead, and wouldn't be anywhere else on earth except right down here in the heart of the barren Antarctic.

And now we were to start paying for our foolhardiness of the first day in removing our snow glasses. All six of us began to get snow blindness, and a miserably disagreeable thing it is, too. The eyes feel as though filled with hot sand. They are continually running and the water freezes on one's cheeks, adding to the discomfort. Frequently there are sharp, stabbing pains, and these grip a person at unexpected moments.

At times we could hardly open our eyes, the glare of the sun on snow and ice was so intense. For miles we often traveled along more by instinct than anything else, trusting to our dogs to help pilot us through. The eye trouble was particularly painful and annoying at noon when we sat down to have a little rest. Opening our eyes to see where our food was, we were dazzled by the brilliant sun which intensified our pain.

Shackleton, who suffered from snow blindness, wrote in his diary, "Snow blindness is a particularly unpleasant thing. One begins by seeing double, then the eyes feel full of grit; this makes them water until one cannot see at all."

At night we used to make applications on each other's eyes with bandages that had a boracic solution in them. This eased the pain considerably. We all had bad cases, although we were fortunate enough not to lose the power of sight altogether for any length of time. Nevertheless, we thought it bad enough, and the trouble stayed with us for weeks.

The expected break in the weather did not come, although it was getting along toward midsummer. The temperature remained low, the wind was bitter and cutting, like a sharp blade. A light hoar-frost continually formed on the surface of the barrier, making both the sledges and our skis drag heavily. As Admiral Byrd says, "It is not generally known that the colder it is, the more difficult the pulling becomes." The dogs, too, were feeling the strain. Our loads were a little bit too much for them. Sometimes a sledge would break through the crust and get on hard snow that was rough, or on a dry, sandy sort of snow that acted like a brake on the sledge runners. More than once sledges would be toppled over and dragged a way before being righted. Luckily our tanks held well and the loads did not come off, even if they loosened up a bit. The dogs had to work hard now and at night they were usually glad to lie still while we fed them, some of them at times too tired to eat their meal until after they had rested a bit.

Day after day we slogged along, many times attaching ropes to the sledges in order to help pull the load, thus doing what we could to ease the weight a little for our faithful dogs. It was hard, back-breaking work, and at night we eagerly sought our sleeping bags after supper. Larry developed blisters on his feet that made it agony for him to take a step, and dressing these at night was a cold job for him.

Despite the fact that the days were so heavily filled, the awful monotony of traveling through the silent land day after day began to wear on us. What's that people say about "still as a mouse?" Even the patter and gnawing of a mouse would have been a relief. When one of the fellows got funny and told of the birds he had heard singing along the trail that day, the rest of us were too lonesome for just such cheerful noises to feel amused by his fairy tales.

We tried every device imaginable to keep our minds off the dull sameness of the job on hand. A quotation from my diary gives a picture of what passes through one's mind while on the march: "The wind is cutting nose and face today. I wish this right eye of mine would quit running. Now my hands are cold. It seems to go in a cycle, face, hands, and feet. Here is another flag (trail marker). There goes my cheek again, frozen stiff. I don't dare open my right eye, for it seems as though a hot wire were in it."

Noon. Tea with lemon powder, a great stimulant. The dogs fall around, dropping in their tracks when a halt is called. The faithful beasts literally work until they drop. At times it is necessary to beat them in order to make them behave, yet they are so willing and friendly.

Under way again. Beginning now to get a little bit warmer. Flag after flag,—we count the miles by these flags. Our legs are getting awfully weary; it seems as though the skis weigh a ton apiece. On we go, moving mechanically, painfully. If only we could drive side by side and have each other's companionship! But that won't work, and we know it. The lead sledge picks the easiest path over the trail and both our dogs and ourselves are saved by following single file. Besides, tired as they are, the dogs would probably try to fight if they were running near each other.

Mile after mile, mile after mile. All white and dead, glittering in the sun. Eyes half closed to keep out the glare and avoid pain. Salty tears running down and freezing in our beards. Mile after mile, mile after mile.

Seems as if we had covered a hundred miles already today. Is Larry walking in his sleep? They call this "summer." Well, maybe! Wonder how it would feel to walk on grass in the shade of green trees? Oh, well, it's a great life if you like it. Mile after mile, mile after— Away ahead Larry jams his ski poles into the snow. Hurrah! That means camp and supper, and then the sleeping bags.

On November 13, a clear, cloudless evening with a temperature twenty-two degress below, we were amazed on coming out of the cook tent to see away to the south in the sky a few degrees above the horizon, a huge distorted mass like a mammoth mountain. This was puzzling because it seemed to be stationary and was deeply gashed and furrowed. Yet it had no visible base. None of us remembered seeing it when we made camp before supper. Finally we realized that this was a mirage, or looming, the same as is found in the desert. This was a reflection of the crevassed area ahead, as though a huge mirror was picturing to us what we would be called on to pass through the next day. Even at that distance of four or five miles it was formidable.

Back in the tent we held a serious talk on what lay ahead. At last Larry remarked, "Well, the advance party warned us of that area we'd have to cross. There will be bad places that can be seen easily, and worse ones hidden under a light roof of snow. We aren't going to lose any dogs or sledges down those bottomless pits if we can help it. What's more, we're not foolish enough to go unprepared for any sort of trouble that may come.

Now, what's your ideas of this layout?" and with that, he sketched several slight changes to be made in our loads and the way we were to proceed.

As a result, the next morning we spent considerable time rearranging the sledges so that each unit was as complete in itself as possible. Thus, if one sledge were lost, we would still have a self-sustaining load. Of course, there was only one radio outfit, but many other tools and instruments were carried in duplicate and no two of these were retained on the same load. Each man carried his share of clothing and food, and the tents were distributed. Alpine rope was taken out for use as life lines.

Our plan was to have the entire party go forward until the edge of the worst part of the crevassed area was reached. There a halt was to be called and a couple of the men left to guard the dogs and sledges. Larry, with the rest of the men, would go ahead to reconnoiter.

It might be that the trail made by the supporting party would be found intact and passable. In that case we would be safe to go through with our sledges loaded as we had them. If the trail was found impassable and a new route had to be cut out, the sledges would have to wait for us to prepare the road for them. Or, it might be, that the old route could be used by observing extra caution and skill.

Well, we would see what lay ahead and plan to adjust ourselves to the conditions as we found them. It might even be necessary to lighten all the loads and go through in relays, making several trips over that awful sector.

After everything was in readiness, we took a short rest before starting out again. This was to be one of the tests of our ability to win through, as we well knew. De Ganahl had radioed from this very section how Walden went down twice into hidden crevasses when making the crossing, and had been pulled out by the alpine rope with which the men had tied themselves together. He had told of being shut in by hollow domes over which every step was made on a thin, trembling roof, and how, crossing a safe-looking ridge, they had found themselves sliding down within ten feet of an open hole, and barely in time managed to turn their teams to a safer part of that mass of knolls and jagged icy peaks.

And so, with what preparations we could make beforehand, we entered these "bad lands" of the barrier that Walden had named "Chasm Pass."

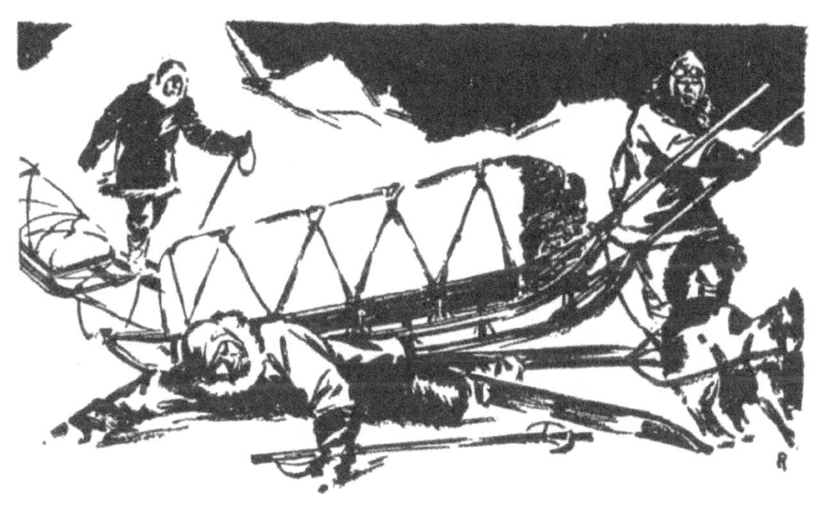

Chapter VII

CREVASSES

WOULD that I could find words to describe this terrifying, weird, yet beautiful, distorted area. As we approached it, a feeling of awe crept over us at the wild picturesqueness of the scene, together with a feeling of concern as to our ability to win through. To be sure, Walden and his party had negotiated it successfully, but we also knew that these vast yawning pits, found throughout this region, were liable to tumble and change without a moment's notice. This sector is one of the mysteries of Antarctica. Why should this particular spot of seven or eight miles in width and maybe fifty to seventy-five miles in length be so torn and distorted?

Slowly we advanced, swinging almost to the east for a couple of miles and then veering back south again, winding in and out between huge ice blocks towering twenty feet and more in the air, or skirting criss-cross chasms. All this time we were gradually climbing. The crevasses were getting bigger, the area more rugged. Finally, on what seemed to be a fairly substantial and sound space, a halt was called. Larry, Mike, Crockett and I went on ahead with a long stretch of alpine rope strung out between us.

The supporting party had placed their flags much closer together here, and it was easy to follow their trail as it zigzagged in and out between crevasses and pits. Fortunately there had not been much action since they had passed through it, and in only two or three places were we forced to detour. Our advance was cautious, but as speedy as possible because we wanted to get through that sector in a day. And so, after about two hours, the four of us came out at last on the south side with a smooth flat barrier stretching before us.

Although extreme caution would have to be exercised, Larry decided that the entire party could make it over that trail without relaying. Taking everything over in one trip meant a big saving in time, and we were all relieved by this decision. So our scouting party hurried back to Norm and Goodale. As soon as lunch was over, we started through.

Here again our dogs proved their ability. Ofttimes a bridge over a crevasse, seemingly strong enough to bear our weight, would break after a sledge had passed over, necessitating a quick command and a prompt turn to avoid plunging the whole of the following units into the black, bottomless pit. As it was, we had accidents enough. Coming down a snow hill, I saw the team ahead run merrily over a big snow bridge and started to take my own team over. But just as I moved out on it, the bridge began to tremble and break. With a wild jump to the side I escaped the falling mass of icy snow that would have carried me down with it. I also managed to slew the dogs around so they were running along the edge of the crevasse. But my ski had caught, I was bowled over, and fell beneath the oncoming sledge. Over the dogs dashed, and the whole weight of the load of the first sledge went over me. But the rear sledge, swung around by the sudden change of direction, went down into the crevasse hanging only by its coupling ropes. In an instant the running dogs slowed down, held back by the tension. It took no word to tell them what had happened. Before I could regain my feet the team had begun hauling slowly and steadily, their bodies close to the snow, until the sledge was hauled up over the edge and was safe on the surface again.

Then, having behaved with more than human sense, they became all dog again and raced wildly away down hill and into another team. Inside of two minutes they had run over me, saved a sledge, and started one of the prettiest little dog fights we had on the whole trip. Mike Thorne, jumping to help, got into a hole of soft snow and disappeared up to his armpits.

For a little while everything was upset. The others

had started back to help, but had to turn their attention to Mike, who was almost buried. Once he was free, the dogs had to be straightened out and given a few lashes to make them behave. Meantime I had scrambled to my feet and was limping ahead, but it wasn't until I changed my clothing that night that I realized that my whole body was a mass of black and blue marks. In fact, it was some time before all those souvenirs of my narrow escape disappeared, and I felt sore and stiff for days. But there was no stopping for a thing like that.

Nor was mine the only casualty. On another occasion, on a downhill slope, with the team running at full speed, a bridged crevasse was reached and a team started over. The weight of the first three dogs broke through the bridge and they were left hanging in midair over the edge of a seemingly bottomless crevasse. Fortunately, the rest of the team stopped and pulled back with an almost miraculous promptness, drawing their unfortunate companions with them, until all of the dogs were on a firm surface again.

There was very little smooth going. About us were deep trenches, ten to thirty feet across, where the ice surface had split open. In other places there were great hollow pits, some covered with icy domes. When the opening was visible, we were fairly safe. Too often it was covered by a thin crust of snow and ice that looked solid and made a veritable trap for the man or dog that ventured on it. Ski poles tested the path before anyone dared try a suspicious hillock, and bridges were crossed with speed in the hope of getting over before they gave way. It was hard, exciting, nerve-wracking work, and although we had entered the area at about half-past eight in the morning, and it was only seven miles through, it was about five o'clock that afternoon before we finally reached the smoother area of the barrier again.

Despite the fact that there were no serious casualties, nor any damage done, we were truly relieved to have that part of the trip behind us. The dogs also seemed to realize what a hazardous journey they had made that day. Too tired to eat, the minute we reached smooth ice and put them on the picket line, they pulled their rations under their paws, safe from possible thieving neighbors, and curled up for a nap before having their meal. Even the irrepressible pups were too tired this night to tease the older dogs. They, too, slumped down wearily to rest. Only Lady's whimpering complaint disturbed the silence, and soon she also fell asleep.

It did not take long to make camp that night. We wanted water, and food, and sleep—but mostly we wanted water! Only our noontime chance to have a drink on all that hard pull. Our mouths were parched and swollen.

After supper Larry sent a radio message to the Admiral telling him that we had passed through the crevassed area without mishap. We knew that all hands at the base were concerned over our safety during this part of the trip, for the supporting party had brought back graphic tales of their own adventures in crossing. So we were mighty happy to be able to report that all was well, for their sakes as well as our own.

Next morning we started on again. Our party was now about one hundred and sixty miles south of Little America, still slogging along, with the temperature away below zero, and the going getting tougher all the time. Always that raw, cutting southeast wind; always the stiffened hands, and faces whitened by frost; the dazzling light throwing its blinding glare back from the glittering barrier floor into our eyes, making them stream and burn constantly. Our breath froze in our beards, forming an icy, loose mask over the lower part of our faces, and we were constantly brushing this ice away.

While the surface was fairly smooth here, we would soon again be having rough going, as well we knew. If the wind and cold continued as bad as we were having them, could we make the mountains and find our way up their difficult passes? The cold slowed us down all the time. Sometimes the temperature would rise a point or two and at once the difference in our speed was noticeable, the pace increasing to fourteen or sixteen miles a day. Again, it would drop, and we would be lucky if we covered five miles. Neither dogs nor men could make speed in the extreme cold or in face of the sharp head wind.

One thing we realized and that was that we must have something to think about during the long, lonely day's work. So it was about this time that we began playing a game with ourselves. In the morning I might decide that that day I was going to take a trip to South America. All day long, when going was easy enough not to demand attention, I would plan the places I'd visit and what I would do there. Or I might decide to revisit some of the places I knew during my school days. Again, I'd pretend I had a million, and all day long I would be busy spending my money.

At night, when we gathered around for a smoke after supper, someone would say, "Well, what did you do today, Obie?" And never a word was there of crevasse and fighting dogs. I'd explain where my million had gone, and then listen while Norm would tell of a tropical trip he had taken, or Larry talk of the specimens he had found on the top of Mt. Nansen, still many miles away. We got a lot of fun out of it all and it kept us from dwelling too much on the worries or discomforts of our trip. We certainly developed active imaginations during those long days, and some of the yarns the fellows would spin were as good as you'd find in any book of adventure.

CHAPTER VIII

COMRADES OF THE AIR

MAN-HAULING with the dogs, struggling over every foot of snow, on the morning of November 18, added only four miles and little encouragement. Fortunately, at noon came one of the greatest thrills of the journey. Every one of us was pretty tired and perhaps a bit discouraged with our lack of progress, when suddenly the low, even purr of motors was heard. Looking up, we beheld the huge tri-motored Ford almost directly over us, and about two hundred feet up in the air. The plane was headed south, evidently going to lay the fuel base at the foot of the mountains, somewhere in the neighborhood of Mt. Nansen, in preparation for the polar flight.

That plane certainly seemed to us a thing of beauty and an inspiration to behold. A vivid manifestation of man's triumph over the obstacles of nature. Out here on this vast, wild solitude, hundreds of thousands of years old, raw and primitive as it was in the beginning, we watched one of science's greatest achievements speed through the still, cold air. Over the scenes of so much misery and hardship suffered by our gallant forerunners in their brave battles in quest of knowledge, it skimmed easily at a rate of a hundred miles an hour. Where others had their discoveries limited to what they could see from the ground, this plane carried a mapping camera that would show the surrounding lands for many hundreds of miles. No mountain could shut off its view, while its accuracy was greater than that of man's eye, since no mirage could deceive it.

In a few moments the plane was out of sight, its soft drone lost in the distance. We stopped a little longer for "ob" that day and started out in the afternoon determined to be worthy of the example of our comrades of the air. Dean Smith was at the controls on that flight, Captain McKinley in charge of aerial photography, Hanson at the radio, and the Admiral in command and also serving as navigator. They told us afterwards that they felt it must have been discouraging to us to see them skim by so quickly and easily, while we had to toil along so slowly and laboriously. But we didn't feel that way about it.

We gloried in their flight and felt a little warmth and comfort in the nearness of other men in this lonely land. And indeed, their passing put new life into us. Still, we needed something to put heart into us that night. We had made only eight miles, although we had all tugged on the ropes with the dogs and Mike and Norm had carried loads on their backs, besides. The mountains seemed very far away. In half a day the plane had carried an immense load of fuel to cache for use on the return from its flight to the Pole, and here we were, scarcely able to get through with just the needed supplies for our trip to the base of the Queen Maud Range. Four hours for them to do what was taking us four weeks!

That night after supper we made contact with Little America by radio and a most disturbing bit of news was given us. No word had been received from the Ford for many hours. The base knew that the plane had reached its objective and deposited its load of extra fuel and food. The return trip northward was more than half completed when suddenly all communication ceased. This meant that the engines had probably stopped, for that would silence the mechanism of the automatic radio transmitter.

This was serious. We did not allow ourselves to think much about a real crack-up, but even a minor mishap in landing or taking off could have destroyed their supplies to the extent of leaving them helpless. The plane was nearer the home base than it was to us, so that if searching parties had to go out, it would be from their end. Unable to rest, we kept in touch with the base for three or four hours, and then turned in for a none too restful sleep.

The next day, although the temperature was a little

above zero and our speed a bit better, the wind was very strong. All told, it was a decidedly disagreeable day. Our thoughts were somewhere out there on the icy plain where perhaps our comrades were in danger.

We made twelve miles that day but the dogs were so tired out that we decided to give them a day of rest. As one of the boys remarked, "What's the good of our feeling fit, if the dogs can't drag along? Better let them have a good breathing spell and then they will be ready to go ahead with new pep, for there isn't a loafer in the whole lot of them." So it was decided to take a day off for rest and going over our gear. Still, that wasn't our chief concern just then.

We hurried getting our radio up that night. Everybody helped, and for once supper became a secondary consideration. All hands sat around in the tiny tent as Fred Crockett tapped out his call for Little America. We were fighting between hope and fear in those few moments before we got them. And then, "Everything O. K." What a relief that short message brought us! Soon we were getting details. The plane had been forced down about eighty miles from camp because of a leaky gas line, but it and its passengers had landed safely. Radio communication had been re-established, and now Balchen had flown the Fairchild to them with an extra gasoline supply, and everything was in order again. What a relief that message was to our little gang away out there near the southern edge of the barrier!

That night the stork visited Belle, one of our lady dogs. Three little huskies came to her and the poor thing did her best to protect them and keep them warm. But it was no use, out there in the wind and cold. They froze to death quickly. Poor Belle! The babies had gone to sleep and never knew what was happening to them, but the poor mother's whimpering kept the other dogs uneasy and fretful all through the night, and that in turn kept us awake most of the night.

We made about fourteen miles the following day, pushing through a miniature snowstorm. The snow fall did not last long and then the sun came out. But the wind held. It had a nasty way of picking up the barrier snow and whirling it about our knees. This skiing in the bright sun with a miniature snowstorm raging for a foot or two above the ground gave us a strange feeling. It had something of the effect of being on a mountain and watching a storm whirling in a valley below.

At noon, just before we stopped for lunch, Belle brought three more pitifully naked bits of life into the world. It was really sad to watch the mother's efforts to save her babies. She looked up at us with the gentlest, most appealing expression, as though to say, "Please help me. I have given you all I have. Can't you save my babies? Look how pretty they are!" Much as we wanted to keep her puppies for her, there was nothing we could do. They could not have survived our long daily marches, and the sledges banged about and sometimes tipped over; so we couldn't carry them that way. The cold again took Belle's babies away from her. Most wonderful of all was to see Belle, after half an hour's rest, take her place in harness once more and pull with all her heart. More and more did we learn to admire the devotion of our dogs and become deeply attached to these wonderful beasts.

It was somewhere about this time that we picked up an unexpected companion. Where he came from and what he lived on there in the heart of the barrier we never could make out, but one day an old skua gull appeared near our camp. For three or four days he followed our trail, much interested in us and our mission. He acted as if he were a penguin, so curious and unafraid was he. He would come so close at times that it is a wonder he didn't form an involuntary breakfast for one of the eager dogs, who looked on him with longing eyes and watering chops. Somehow he managed to keep clear, and after a few days disappeared into the void from which he had come, and was not seen again, although we all kept on the lookout for him.

As we tramped along we wondered how much longer it would take to get to the mountains. The dogs were rested by the day of leisure we had allowed them and were pulling ahead like good fellows. We had an idea that most of the remainder of the way to the mountains would be over flat and unbroken surface, but in that we were wrong. We had a couple of days travel over fairly smooth surface and then encountered some of the roughest going we were to meet on the southward trip. Evidently, where the barrier met the edge of the land there was considerable disturbance.

After the Ford plane got back to Little America, we

had a message telling us that they had sighted countless snow-clad peaks to the southward beyond Axel Heiberg.

"Great peaks, some of them showing dark rocks and many glaciers," Petersen radioed to us. "They photographed the area they passed over and saw beyond the Axel Heiberg Glacier, Liv Glacier, Mt. Nansen, and sighted the Queen Maud Range." So there *were* mountains down there ahead of us! If we had been impatient to reach the mountains before, we were positively "rarin' to go" with this news to make us more anxious to see what lay down there beyond the end of the barrier ice.

CHAPTER IX

LAYING TRAIL

MILES out now, the barrier surface was getting rougher and rougher. It was ridged by the winds in regular corrugations much like the small dunes found along sandy beaches. These formations are called *sastrugi*. Varying in height from one to eight inches, they occur in regular waves that range from a foot to three or four feet from crest to crest. And these crests are of ice, usually slightly hooked at the edge, so that in walking "against the waves," the ski-tips were often caught on these hooks, with a resultant heavy fall.

With this bumpy surface to slide over, and with the snow dry and sticky, we had a real job on our hands.

Time and again we stumbled and skidded, often falling directly under our sledges, with the result that there was many a bruised shin in the crowd. It was hard work to keep our tempers from showing bruises, too, at times. But our dogs battled on determinedly, although tails were drooping, and many an animal showed his weariness now.

Curious illusions began to be experienced. We were forced to keep our eyes glued on a spot directly ahead of our skis. After a few hours of this one felt as though he were passing through a canyon with white walls hemming him in on both sides. This was partly because our glasses showed everything dark in our direct line of vision, but the glaring white of the barrier snow was always visible out of the corners of our eyes. Sometimes the canyon walls melted into a milky river flowing along past us, but always we had that sense of being shut in so that we couldn't look to one side. If we did turn our heads, again we saw what was directly before our eyes, and there were those white barriers hiding what lay to either side.

It is quiet, always quiet, on a march like this. The soft crunching of the snow under the dogs' pads and the sledge runners are the only sounds that break the stillness, except when, with a boom like the discharge of a great cannon, there is a break in the barrier ice and a new crevasse is born. It gets to be wearing, does this silence, and the monotony and loneliness of our surroundings was one of the most difficult features of our lives out there. Instead of growing used to it, we felt it more and more as time went on. No wonder we welcomed the companionship and the idle chatter that came with the supper hour at the end of each day. Those foolish games we played with ourselves during the day made talk enough at night, and sometimes brought about a real argument. I remember once when Freddie told of how he had spent a big sum of money that day, we all jumped on him for not having spent it differently. He let us talk on for a while and then came back with, "Well, if you guys know more than I do about spending a hundred thousand, suppose you all try it tomorrow and see if you can do so much more with it."

So the next day as we marched along, guiding our dogs and seemingly just following a lonesome trail, our dreams were on our home towns where we were spending a fortune with lavish hand. Of course we all thought we had done better than Freddie, and also, of course, Fred didn't agree with us, but at least another day had gone by, and we were nearly twenty miles nearer the distant mountains.

By this time we had passed some distance beyond the badly crevassed area and also had gone beyond the two hundred mile trail laid out for us by the advance party. At last we were completely "on our own." There was nothing ahead to guide us. Our trail had to be laid out as we went ahead, making always for the Queen Maud mountains that lay beyond the far end of the barrier ice.

Now progress was more difficult, because time had to be taken to mark trail for the return trip. The flags that we had brought with us were broken out from our sledge loads, and every half mile we marked trail. Where going was hard we sometimes put the flags still closer together. At the end of every fifty miles we made a cache, storing food and some other supplies in houses we built of roughly-hewn and squared snow blocks. These served as food caches as well as snow beacons, but because of the latter use they were sometimes built as high as fifteen to twenty feet before being topped with our larger orange colored flags. Fortunately for us we did not have any of these caches melt down enough to spoil the food supplies, a misfortune that Amundsen suffered on his polar trip. By having these tall beacons along our route, our return path was marked and also provided with stores of food for the return trip. This lightened our outgoing loads in some measure. Moreover, we had to remember that one of our duties was to stand by for the flight to the Pole. In case of disaster and wreck, the men in the plane might find our marked trail and cached supplies a real life-saver. If accident came where we could reach the party, the lighter our loads and the better victualed the return route, the easier our task would be.

One experiment in marking was to color the heaped snow piles with analine dyes, making the whole mound appear in color instead of merely having an orange flag flying from its peak. Several different colors were tried with the idea of studying the effect on our return journey. It was about this time also that we noticed quite an interesting phenomenon. With the temperature far below zero and at times with our cheeks frozen stiff, some particles on the canvas sledge tanks would be melting, showing the intensity of the direct rays of the sun. There was to be an amusing near-tragedy that turned to comedy as result of this phenomenon, but we had no suspicion of it as we watched little rills of water dropping from the loads piled up on our sledges.

Visibility was poor. Several times the dogs seemed uncertain of the way. If anything went wrong with the compass by which Larry navigated, we might have a serious time picking up our trail on the return march. The disaster that brought death to Captain Scott was a constant reminder to us that every precaution was worth taking. And so, now that we were marking our own trail in more and more difficult surroundings, we made allowance for the possibility of losing our way. It meant plenty of work. At every fifty-mile depot, while the rest of the fellows were busy about camp after supper, Mike and I, who had volunteered for this duty, since we were the official surveyors, put on our skis again and set out to lay down east and west markers. For five miles on either side of the main north and south trail we placed orange flags at intervals of a half mile. This was in case that, by any mishap, we got off the main trail we could pick up one of these wing markers and thus find our way back. The flags were identified by an *E* or *W* and a number to indicate distance and direction. In this way we could tell how far we were from our main trail and in which direction it lay. The supporting party had done this work at each fifty mile depot as far as they went, but now it was up to Mike and me to lay these markers. It was cold work but there was always one consolation, for Larry thoughtfully had big mugs of steaming hot soup awaiting us when we got back to camp, cold, tired, and hungry.

On November 22, after making seventeen miles, we reached our Number Five depot, located two hundred and forty-three miles from Little America. We were all quiet at supper that night. This was one of the times that Mike and I were glad we were surveyors. The ten miles extra skiing was welcomed and we set out with a feeling of thankfulness for our job. For to Norman Vaughan fell the sad duty of killing five of our dogs that had weakened. Larry had begun his supper, and then had put down his cup of cocoa on the food box with, "There is no use trying to put it off any longer. It is better to destroy those dogs than let them suffer. And the others need fresh meat to keep them going. I'm not going to order anyone to kill them. I know how hard it is for a driver to do that to any of his own team; so I'm open for suggestions."

Before any of us could say anything, Norm spoke up quickly, "See here, Larry, inasmuch as none of those dogs belong to my team, and also as I have had more or less charge of the dogs since starting out from the base, I think it is only fair for me to do this job."

It was a generous proffer on Norm's part, for he loved the dogs as well as any of us did. We all offered to relieve him of the sad task, but he stood firm in his belief that it was really a part of his duty, and Larry finally agreed with him.

So a little white wall of snow was erected about fifty feet from the camp and it was behind this screen that the animals were shot. The rest seemed to sense what was to happen as soon as one of the doomed dogs was led away, and they would all start to whimper. At the crack of the shot, the dogs on the picket line jumped up and barked frantically. It was tragic for us all. Not a dog of the lot but was a real friend. Yet—it was simply the law of survival. Those poor animals would not have survived much longer and it was kinder to shoot them than to let them die off.

The loss of these dogs forced us to cut down to four teams. We divided the remaining supplies equally, adjusting the loads according to the strength of the dogs. This left Mike Thorne without a team and he was free to give all his time to being point man. His splendid ability on skis made him an ideal person for this job. He would get about a hundred yards ahead of us and sort of break trail. Larry, now steering along with the first team, which had the boat compass lashed on the top of the load, would call out to Mike, "Right!" or "Left!" as the case might be, and thus keep Mike pointing in the desired direction. In this manner we navigated, and it was wonderful to see the way Mike kept a straight course. The dogs seemed to travel better, too. It was like having a pace-maker for a track athlete.

November 25th stands out in memory as a very hard day. With the temperature at three above zero and a twenty-five mile wind cutting our faces like a ragged-edged knife, with the flashing sun causing our eyes to burn and smart and water constantly, we pushed along steadily. Although tired to the point of exhaustion, that night was one of jubilation when we looked at the sledge-meter and found that we had covered a bit more than twenty miles. Cutting out the dogs that had been unable to keep the pace and putting Mike out to lead the way had evidently speeded us up considerably.

This spurt had brought us to Depot Number Six. That meant east and west flags again. So, after supper, while the others sat about kidding us on the hard life of a surveyor, Mike and I took our extra hike, five miles east and five miles west. Both of us were more than ready to "call it a day" when we had each covered ten extra miles on our job that night.

It was not only the wind and sun and that extra "flag day celebration," as one of the fellows unfeelingly called our extra survey job, that made that day memorable. We had reached the point where one hard day seemed a good deal like another hard day and was taken as a matter of course. But it was on this day that Mike, topping a small ridge, had suddenly waved wildly and begun what looked like a crazy dance on skis. We wondered what had happened, but didn't have long to wait.

"The mountains! See 'em? We're getting there at last!"

All speeded forward and stood looking off into the dim distance. Yes, there were the mountains we had come all this way to find. Indistinct, for they were still a hundred miles distant, but it was cheering to have our goal appear at last. We had come two hundred and ninety miles from our base and another hundred miles of barrier ice had yet to be crossed, but it was reassuring actually to see these great peaks ahead.

Like a huge billow of clouds, the mountains lay stretched on the far horizon. And almost in the center of the range loomed, high above the rest, the flat, massive tableland summit of Mt. Nansen. This was the mightiest of them all, towering skyward almost eighteen thousand feet.

As the sun lowered and swung around to the southern sky line, the jagged profile of peaks become more distinct. There they loomed across our path like a huge wall, seemingly defying all man's puny strength. It was going to be a serious task to scale those slopes, yet that was one of the objects with which we had set forth. At any rate, the view of those peaks gave us something to think about as we slogged along all that day.

The day had been fairly warm, and the rose tints of the mountain peaks had promised something of mildness for the days to come. At least, so it seemed to us. And then, after that scene of loveliness, the ever-changing southland spoke again that night when a terrific blizzard struck us shortly after camp had been made. It certainly was one bit of good luck that the dogs had all been fed and bedded for the night, and that tents were safely up and aprons fastened down by the piled snow.

Larry had been out with his shovel, taking off the surface snow before digging up the cleaner layer beneath to melt for our drinking water, when the blow struck.

We all made a dive for the tents. We had supper and

lay about the cook tent for a while, talking about what we would have when we got back to base camp. My recollection is that good hot baths and clean shaves were about the most popular forms of amusement suggested, though there was some talk of food other than "hoosh" and granite-hard biscuits.

Then we crawled off to our sleeping tents, and wasn't it good to lie snug and comfortable, hearing the roar of the wind and the rattle of hard snow pellets against the walls of the tents!

The blow continued all night and in the morning we had to bend almost double against it to reach the cook tent. For the first time since starting out we took our ease at breakfast. No use fighting against this sort of storm! To try it would be to court losing our way, and possible death in some crevasse or other hidden danger.

Much as we would ordinarily have welcomed a holiday, the sight of the mountains goaded us to reach our destination. For once there was little joy in having time to loaf. So our relief was great when the wind let up a bit and Larry suggested that we try to get under way about noon.

Luckily, the morning's rest had put new energy into both men and dogs. We needed it! It was all we could do to keep going. The wind, that had died down a bit, soon grew stronger again and fairly cut the skin on our faces. If it had not been that it was only one degree above zero we never would have been able to stand it. Time and again we had to throw our arm across our cheeks to ease the sting, stumbling along by peering be-

At the beginning
of the long day's
grind the dogs
were alert and
eager to be off

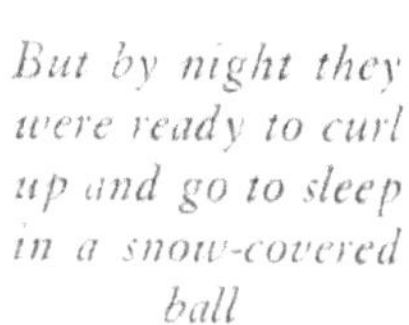

But by night they
were ready to curl
up and go to sleep
in a snow-covered
ball

Arthur Walden was
a veteran dog man
who had charge of
the dogs of the Expe-
dition and led the
supporting party that
laid bases for us

neath the shield of a bent elbow. Then our hands would get cold and we would have to warm them, letting our faces take the icy blasts. When you turn your head to avoid the wind you lose your sense of balance on the rough surface, skis slip out from under and you take a tumble. I was struggling along with one eye closed and barely peeping out of the other, for the snow blindness still pained and made me weep big tears that froze on my cheeks as they fell. Oh, well, when it wasn't one thing, it was another! That's all part of the life of an explorer in the Antarctic.

Looking back, it seems to me that this day, November 25th, and the day before were about the two hardest ones we had had up to that time. Yet, despite wind and cold we managed to cover twelve and a half miles before making camp, but we suffered every inch of the way. Even the dogs seemed to crouch low, as if to escape the bitter winds. They found it hard to breathe, just as we men did, for the wind fairly strangled one. With all the air in the world about them, they almost smothered at times, and we had to rest them every mile or two.

No time was wasted in making camp when we drew to a halt, and the dogs curled down in the snow at once, ready for a nap before eating. We never got over our wonder at the way those animals made themselves comfortable in their beds of snow and could sleep through a blizzard as comfortably outdoors as we did inside our wind-proof tents.

Snuggled deep in our sleeping bags that night, a voice floated out from the other tent, "And next time I go on any sort of expedition, I'm going to sign up with a leader who wants to explore the tropics. I'm going where there ain't no wind, and ain't no snow, and ain't no blizzard, and where the little flowers bloom the year round, and—"

"Aw, forget it!" That was Norm. "After you've had a good night's sleep, you'll just love the pretty snow and ice. And you can't have pemmican and 'hoosh' in the tropics. *You* don't know when you're well off, boy. Try sleep for what ails you."

There was a laugh, and then all was still. Only the moan of the wind and sharp reports, as of artillery fire, when the ice cracked near us.

CHAPTER X

THE POLAR FLIGHT

EXPECTATIONS are high these days. Orders to stand by for the polar flight are certain to come soon. At our end of the line the weather has been good for flying, but we realize that it may be less satisfactory near the base camp. There has been no word from the Admiral, although every day at noon we stop and get the radio working in order to pick up any instructions. Until this time we have been content to put up the radio every second night, but with time growing shorter, we signal for orders each day.

That flight means much to us and our plans, for if anything goes wrong with the plane we may have to turn ourselves into a rescue party and give up all thought of the geological work on which we started out. Still, that isn't as important as having the plane make its objective and fly safely back, for the biggest event of our expedition is the reaching of the South Pole by airplane. All else is secondary.

Meantime the mountains were beckoning us on. Always they seemed so near when we started out in the morning, and yet when night came they were no nearer, as far as we could see.

Yet despite our desire to push forward and gain those elusive peaks of blue ice, on the morning of November 27th, we enjoyed the luxury of an extra hour of sleep. At half past nine that morning, while the rest of us reveled in glorious laziness and smoked an extra cigarette over our tea in the cook tent, Crockett called the base. With his Morse code dots and dashes he asked for instructions, and in a couple of minutes he was back with a message for Larry. "This looks like the big day in camp," he commented, handing the written message over to our boss.

Larry read it aloud. "Will you please give us hourly weather reports?" A commonplace enough sentence, perhaps, but it was from the Admiral and meant that the moment had come for the supreme test of aviation, if weather conditions remained favorable.

There was no harnessing of dogs and getting under way that morning. Instead, the animals enjoyed their extra rest while we men killed time speculating on different phases of the big hop until "ob," which we celebrated with an extra ration of chocolate. Each hour

Fred clicked off his weather report until half-past one. When he got camp on the ether again at that hour there came back a message that was snappy and to the point. "Bad weather here. No flying."

So that was that! We all felt a bit disappointed, but realized that the plane must not start except under the best of conditions. There was no more excuse for lolling about camp this day. Freddie went out to pack up his radio, and the rest of us, with great effort, shook off the feeling of comfortable laziness that had crept over us during our morning of idleness, broke camp, and got under way at about three o'clock so that the day would not be at total loss.

In order to make up for lost time, we traveled until half-past eleven that night, making a good twenty miles. During that march the sun lay to the south, just over the big mountain range. It was the most awe-inspiring and glorious sight that any of us had ever witnessed. All day the snowy peaks had glittered and gleamed ahead of us, and as the sun moved round behind them and was hidden from us, the snows assumed the most marvelous combinations of delicate color one could think of. Pale gray, pink and blue, so perfectly blended that the whole world before us seemed unreal. That beautiful picture to the south held us spellbound. We would stand around while making camp just watching the ever-changing shadows on the slopes as they turned to lavender and purple tints, while above, the peaks glowed rose-pink in the brighter light. That view alone was worth the entire sixteen hundred mile trek.

The next day, November 28, the weather was perfect, and we knew the flight was not to be held up much longer. It was Thanksgiving Day; so we slept late while awaiting orders. Sure enough, shortly after breakfast there was a message from the base, saying that the weather there was good, despite some light clouds. The plane would take off in a few hours if conditions at our end were good. Larry radioed back that all looked favorable, from our position, near the Queen Maud Range.

Then they asked if we wanted anything special, adding, "You may not get it, you know. Besides, it has to be small, for the plane is loaded to the last pound it is able to carry."

There wasn't much discussion about what we wanted! Any news from home and some cigarettes. If I remember correctly, some of the fellows listed cigarettes first!

And so we lounged around on this holiday, making repairs on our gear and clothing, both of which were beginning to show signs of hard wear. About half-past twelve Larry yelled at us to come for our turkey dinner. The turkey was nothing but the same old "hoosh," as usual, but this was topped off with an extra ration of strawberry jam in celebration of the day.

We were beginning to wonder whether the weather was again holding the plane from starting when, at four o'clock Fred yelled at us, "Radio says the plane has just taken off!"

That must have been a great moment in Little America. The plans of years, the peak of aviation advancement was under test now. The thoughts and well wishes of millions throughout the world were with the *"Floyd Bennett"* as it disappeared in the gray sky on its history-making flight. We, on our part, felt a special jubilation: ours was the chance to see the plane nearer the object of its flight than could any others.

In a few moments Crockett made himself comfortable on his sleeping bag, adjusted his head-set and tuned in. Soon the loud steady roar of the three powerful motors could be heard. He tuned his set lower so as to be easy on his ears and settled down for an extended vigil. As long as that roar continued he knew that all was well.

The rest of us could hear nothing of all this; so we fed the dogs and busied ourselves at different things for an hour or two. Gradually we started casting glances toward the northern sky line. It was rather too much to expect that the plane would pass directly over us. If it did, the altitude would probably be so high that we would have difficulty picking the men out. Still, though we kept assuring each other that we would be lucky to catch even a distant glimpse of the plane, we all hoped to get a fleeting view of its passing.

And then, at about ten minutes after seven, Crockett called from his tent, "the motor is much louder. It must be getting close now."

All of us strained our eyes up into that cloudless northern sky, and sure enough, away to the north and west of us a dark speck appeared. It was flying low and they were evidently looking for us. Just about the time we caught sight of them, they must have spotted our orange colored tents, for they suddenly swung directly

toward us. Bigger and bigger the dark spot grew.
Although a surface north wind of about ten mile velocity
had sprung up, they were making good time, possibly
a hundred miles an hour. In a few minutes they roared
above us at about fifteen hundred feet. We must have
been a funny sight, gaping up into the sky, waving our
arms and shouting words we knew they could not hear.

Someone could be distinguished at the side window,
but we were not able to make out who it was. Probably
McKinley, taking a picture of our camp. We could not
even glimpse the others. By radio they called Crockett
and got our exact latitude and longitude, so that they
could make a check on their instruments.

A small white object dropped through the trapdoor
in the floor of the plane. It spread larger and larger, as
a tiny parachute opened and drifted slowly downward
to land quite near us.

That was all. They were gone, climbing swiftly to
gain altitude for the hop over the mountain range. We
rushed out and picked up the parachute with its attached
tin they had dropped to us. It contained some cigarettes;
photographs of the spot where they had established their
fuel base, so that we could find it if need arose; home
news and a note from the Admiral. One other note
we found. This was from our aerologist, Harrison,
giving us the football scores that they had just received
from the United States. It seemed funny to sit way out
there so many thousands of miles from all civilization,
and have the late news flashes from home. Quite as
exciting was the realization that this news had been

brought us by the men who would within an hour or two be flying over the South Pole.

We watched the plane move farther and farther away toward the south until it disappeared in the shining haze above the peaks. Yes, there was plenty of work and minor disappointments to endure, but we certainly felt that a tiny share of the making of world history was ours that day, and this atoned for many a discomfort.

Now they were gone, and again we settled down to the long watch. Crockett could still hear the hum of the motors and knew that all was well. About an hour after the plane had passed over us, Larry yelled for all hands to come to supper. One of us relieved Crockett at the radio while he ate. The same steady roar kept coming in over the air, an assurance that they were still flying onward. We tried to keep ourselves occupied as best we could but somehow were not able to concentrate very well. Our minds and thoughts were with those four speeding southward. An then, shortly after midnight I was able to write in my diary, "12:20 a. m. Just heard the base radio congratulations to the plane. So they must have made it. We are glad. Now remains their big job of getting back safely."

We gave Crockett a resting spell again. Although Fred had been at the radio most of the past day and had listened steadily since four in the afternoon, except for his brief supper respite, after a short rest he said he would carry on again for the remainder of the night. So the rest of us promptly hit the hay, after getting his promise to call us if anything unusual happened.

When we woke at about seven in the morning, Fred was still on the job. He had dozed a little now and then, but even so was hearing the monotonous motor roar in his ears. Any change in that sound would have wakened him promptly. We breakfasted and proceeded to break camp, all except the radio tent. Then we sat around waiting for word that the plane had completed its return trip and landed safely, after which we could go on. Its return had been by a slightly different route; so we knew that only the nearness and distance of the engine roar would give an idea of its location.

At the end of a twenty hour watch we were signed off at eleven o'clock. Little America reported the safe return of the plane and its personnel. Happy that the flight had been successful, we packed up the radio tent and got under way. While it meant traveling until late that night, we kept going until we had covered twenty-three miles. Of course, it didn't get dark; so the going wasn't harder at night than in the daytime. And we just *had* to reach those mountains! Larry had said, "It's the mountains or bust today." But the distances are very deceptive in that clear atmosphere, with nothing to relieve the whiteness and help mark the miles. Although the range grew bigger and bigger, the mountains were a long way off when we quit and made camp.

Chapter XI

ICE BRIDGES AND GLACIERS

AGAIN the cry, "The mountains or bust today sure!" And we were off for another day of trekking. That big, somber mass seemed so close, how could we fail to attain its base in a few hours? Yet before we were to reach these mountains we were to experience the hardest and most thrilling day of that entire trip.

Starting off early and with weather clear and the going good, our progress seemed satisfactory and rapid. At noon "ob" our estimate was that we would reach the base of the range at about six o'clock. Under way again, the sledges had gone only a short distance when small cracks in the ice were noticed. These gradually got larger and larger. About three o'clock we had reached a sector where the surface became quite rolling and icy. Real crevasses began to appear, hundreds of feet long and thinly bridged. At the same time a strong south wind sprung up, whirling the snow up from the ground all around us. It was difficult to see, due to the flying snow, although the sun was shining brightly.

The dogs started slipping into the edges of the crevasses. Time and again two or three would go through, only their harness saving them from pitching into the black depths. Each time they were deftly pulled out by their mates, who backed away until those that had gone over the edge were hauled up again. The dogs sensed the danger that we all faced and at once started to execute a maneuver that made us love them more than ever. Without a word of command, when they came to a crevasse they would turn and cross it sharply at right angles instead of running along on it. This they might easily have done, since many ice bridges were quite wide. But by cutting straight across they managed to get over before the thin spans had time to crumble under their weight, never keeping us on those trembling bridges longer than was healthful.

Conditions were becoming more and more trying. The quick rushes across sixty to seventy foot chasms that had no bottom, the stinging snow cutting our faces, and hiding the dangers at our very feet wore us all out. Yet the huge mass of mountains, appearing at moments when the air cleared, lured us on, even while they fooled us with their seeming nearness.

Larry had said, "Well, we just have to make those mountains or bust today," and more than once we wondered if we wouldn't "bust." Still, on we went, determined to reach our goal before we quit that day. So we marched, and we marched, and we marched, threading our way between and over hundreds and hundreds of blind crevasses, feeling the ice bridges breaking under us as we leaped for life. Our nerves began to get jumpy. When we reached a spot that seemed fairly solid we would stop for a few minutes to rest ourselves and our dogs, but we never stopped for long.

The surface now became solid blue. We were moving over glacier ice that had poured down through the mountain passes and spread out over the barrier floor. It was a wonderful sight, this deep blue translucent floor, but Ed growled unfeelingly, "We could do with a little less beauty and a little more safety."

The sledges would not track. We went sloughing and swinging from side to side. Our skis did not always help us, for our feet shot out from under us constantly, and we went down on the hard surface. Sometimes we struck a small hummock and shot wildly into the air before landing on the ice with a force that proved the surface was solid enough for any weight hereabouts. Even the dogs found no traction on the slippery ice and slid about badly. They tried to claw in, but there was nothing for them to hold on to. At last, with the dogs staggering in their harness, their strength almost worn out, and ourselves at the point of mental and physical exhaustion, almost dead on our feet we slid across a fairly solid section of ice that was not as heavily crevassed as the rest. And there, in the shadow of the towering mountains and at the foot of Liv Glacier we called a halt and made camp for the night. We had "reached the mountains" all right, but came pretty close to "busting" in doing it.

Without question, this had been by far our most trying day. So exhausted were we that we made no attempt to get supper, being content with a piece of chocolate. Even the dogs were too tired to eat, flopping down in their places on the picket line, utterly spent. For the first time those young fellows, Cocoa, Sky, Al Smith, and Kit had had enough. Although they nibbled at their food, there was not the usual ravenous rush, and they were very ready to call it a day. Most of their ration was saved to eat later in the night when they had rested.

We slept late the next morning. A strange outfit we must have looked as we huddled around the primus stove in the morning for breakfast. A month's growth of beard bristled from our faces and the wind and cold had tanned and blistered us until we all could exhibit several combinations of complexion. Pink where the frozen skin had peeled off leaving the new underskin exposed; tan from the cutting wind; whiskers of black or red; hair growing long and unkempt, with streaks of grease or dirt here and there. Right then we could easily have got jobs scaring little children to bed. Larry looked us over and remarked with conviction, "Well, if we fellows can't find any other jobs when we get back to the States, I'm sure some farmers will be glad to hire us as scarecrows."

This day was warm, and what a relief that was after the cold and biting winds we had been fighting the last few days. The lower foothills were almost entirely free of snow because of the intensity of the sun's rays, and their bare rocky faces radiated the heat. No furs were needed here. In fact, some of us were comfortable in undershirts. It is strange to think of heat down there, over three hundred miles nearer the Pole than was Little America. However, as everything is relative, what we called "heat" was really but a bit warmer than the bitter cold we had but shortly before experienced. Up in the United States people would rightfully have considered that we were experiencing quite nipping winter weather.

Both the dogs and ourselves needed a good rest, our gear required overhauling after the rough treatment it had received in crossing the crevasses; so we decided to get our second wind before moving camp again. Besides, we were to do some survey and exploration work here at the end of the barrier ice, for this was really the shore line of the Ross Barrier. We had now been out twenty-nine days, and felt we might take it a little easy.

That did not mean inactivity. Quite the contrary. "Taking it easy" meant that our tents stayed where they were for a few days and the dogs were permitted a real rest. About ten o'clock on the morning following our arrival, Larry, Mike and I outfitted ourselves with alpine rope, ice axes and a bit of lunch and started up the glacier. This was literally a river of ice, flowing slowly down from the high tableland beyond and emptying into the barrier ice. But where water would have flowed swiftly, the movement of a glacier can be counted in inches each year. The three men who remained in camp busied themselves repairing our gear before they rested.

The immensity of the place almost appalled us, but Larry was as delighted as a child at the prospect of getting to work and perhaps finding some fossils. We had been puzzled by the distant view of the glacier, for it had seemed all spotted with black dots through its river of ice. Now, climbing its surface, we found that these black spots were great boulders that had been washed down from the heights and gradually imbedded in the ice flow. A few protruded, but many were altogether under the surface of the ice.

Luckily we had thought to put crampons on our feet. The ice was so bare that it would have been impossible to stand had it not been for these steel spikes fastened under our boots. The glacier proved to be very heavily crevassed and much more care than usual had to be exercised because we were without the protection of our ski runners. We stretched our rope so as to allow about seventy feet between us and made it fast under our arms. With skis our weight would have been distributed over a long surface, but now our entire weight came down flat with each step. It gave us a strange feeling to walk out on a bridged crevasse, the edges of which were crumbling, and realize that at any moment the whole thing might crush under us. In comparison with the swift gliding of skis, this slow walking over one of these snow arches seemed to consume ages.

Visibility was poor and distance again deceived us.

The dogs were a marvelous lot, and no one could help loving them, for their keen intelligence was often responsible for saving us from many bad situations

We could not but feel insignificant with Mount Nansen of the Queen Maud Range towering over 16,000 feet above us

Our intention had been to go to the top of the ice flow, but two o'clock found us not more than a third of the way. So we stopped for a bite to eat and then were forced to start our return. This work of getting down was almost harder than getting up and made us so warm that we all stripped to our very undershirts, but on reaching the barrier floor we found the wind so sharp and brisk that we lost no time in piling our clothes back on.

Evidently we couldn't rely on appearances in this queer land. The next day Mike and I measured off a two-mile base line in front of the glacier mouth and did quite a bit of survey work. We shot angles from either end and from these determined the glacier to be about eight and a half miles wide. Only in that manner could we determine the width and height of that elusive glacier. At supper that night Larry said, "We have the general lay of this land now and we can do just so much and no more in the time we have for this trip. So let's head southeast tomorrow, follow along the range, pick up the fuel base made by the plane, and then on to Axel Heiberg Glacier. Our work had better be concentrated on it and on Mt. Nansen."

He was the leader and what he said went with the rest of us. Anyway, we were anxious to move on. One job remained. That first mountain camp had to be named. Everyone had bright ideas, but nobody was impressed by the other fellows' suggestions until someone said, "Why not name it after Cyclone?" That ended the discussion. We all agreed that as this was the coldest and windiest of mountain camps it rightfully should bear the name of our weather man back in Little America, Bill Haines. And Camp Haines it is to this day.

The next morning we broke camp and headed southeast, keeping in fairly close to the mountains as the ice cracks proved less large and frequent the nearer we held to the range. The wind picked up after an hour and once more the snow whirled around us viciously. The mountains served as a good guide, the surface was fairly solid, and so we kept going. With the sun shining through this maelstrom it looked as if the barrier was smoking. Great waves of this snow "smoke" whirled upward, to disappear in the air above.

One of the things that relieved the boredom of sledging all day was the ever-changing, ever-interesting impressions and conditions one encountered. On that particular day, for instance, the wind got up to about twenty-five miles an hour, which is a pretty brisk breeze to buck against. At the same time, the temperature was high, and we had neither storm nor cold to fight. So we made good time, clicking off sixteen miles before night.

CHAPTER XII

GEOLOGY ANTARCTICA

TWENTY-THREE miles of sledging on December fifth brought us to the mouth of the west branch of the huge Axel Heiberg Glacier. At last we were in the very shadow of the majestic old Mt. Nansen. Now, the sun's rays, reflecting heat from the bare rocks, made traveling very warm.

Despite snow and ice around us, the sun, shining directly down for so many hours each day and never quite disappearing at night, kept us conscious that December is the heart of antarctic summer. We failed at this time to find the cache that the aviators had left on their first trip south. It was not where we expected, and so pushed on, not wanting to lose any time in search,

131

since we had no real need of any of the supplies we might have found there.

The day after we reached the mouth of the glacier was spent building a big cache out of snow blocks. After the cache was ready came the job of checking and storing most of our food there before making the ascent. No use carrying more than necessary up those crags, for we were bent on climbing the glacier to its top and reaching Mt. Nansen, beckoning to us from the distance. We took two weeks' supplies on our sledges, leaving the rest in the cache at our base. This camp was named "Strom," in honor of Sverre Strom, the man who had helped make those light-weight sledges that were serving us so well.

Then, with three seven-dog teams, we headed up the glacier, bent on reaching Mt. Nansen, where Larry wanted to study the formation and hunt for any fossils that might supply traces of early animal or vegetable life in that part of the world. In certain parts of Antarctica, other explorers had discovered lichens and mosses that had been embedded in sand or earth, and in the course of ages had turned to stone. If such specimens could be found on Mt. Nansen, they would help show that at one time, ages ago, there had been life where now all was ice and snow.

Would we make the top of that frozen waterfall that was known as Axel Heiberg Glacier? More than once doubt assailed us, but there, a little way beyond the glacier top, was Mt. Nansen sparkling in the sunlight and beckoning us on. We had started with the knowledge that this would be one of the hardest pulls we had yet had, but we were rewarded, for it proved to be one of the most interesting days of our journey.

It didn't take long to realize that it was lucky our loads had been cut down, for ours was a steady up-hill pull. At about three thousand feet we got into a fog of low-hanging clouds. Such a chilling, penetrating fog as it was! Seemed to work through our clothes and flesh to chill our very bones. Ugh, that fog! And through it we climbed that sloping river of ice, slippery, yet with rough ice ridges hidden at times under the snow so that stumbling over them was the first intimation we had that they were there. Besides, the whole glacier was cut by great crevasses. Luckily these ran up and down instead of across the surface and we did not have to cross them. Still, we were forced to dodge around and skirt them. Doing this was hard enough in clear weather. In the fog, climbing those icy slopes, it certainly kept us from being bored that day. Sometimes a low-hanging cloud would swirl about us and we would have to stand still until it passed, lest we step off into some hidden crevasse. We went on until forty-one hundred feet above sea level had been reached. Then we camped, thankful that men, dogs, and sledges had come through safely thus far. This place was named Camp Balchen, in honor of the famous aviator and other member of the sledge building crew.

This business of camping on a glacier wasn't so easy. A fairly level spot had to be found, one big enough to take care of the dogs comfortably. They took the matter calmly and slept as well in that high altitude as they had in cozier quarters. For that matter, we men also slept well, tired from the day's strain of skirting gaping gashes that had no visible bottom, and making headway through a veil of fog.

Next morning, under way again early, forty-seven hundred feet elevation was reached at noon. Our first objective had been reached, for this day we lunched at the foot of a steep ice fall that poured down like Niagara from somber old Nansen.

After lunch, Larry proposed that Mike, Fred, and Goodale go up this ice fall and on over toward the lower levels of Nansen to help him hunt for rock samples. Norm and I were left behind to make camp.

As soon as the four men had stuffed their pockets with the little canvas bags marked in big black letters, "L. M. GOULD. GEOLOGICAL SPECIMENS," and had started on their quest, Norm and I hauled our sleeping bags out and propped them against the sledges. These made comfortable couches on which we spent the afternoon in writing and basking in the sun. How small and unimportant we felt amid that silent spectacle of grandeur! Here, over four thousand feet up, great peaks about us reached so much higher that we seemed at the bottom of an abyss. Flat tops and sharp peaks, the mountains rose about us, and from them poured great rivers of deep, solid ice. Snow and ice encrusted everything. Again we felt the awe of being in a dead land. There was something eerie in being the only living creatures in the midst of these great peaks.

We got quite a kick out of being the first group of men ever to penetrate these regions. Our voices and the dogs' cries were the first to shatter the silence of thousands of years. Every once in a while the sun would be hidden by clouds. Instantly the warmth would change to bitter cold. A few moments later the sun burst forth again and we would shed the fur parkas we had hurriedly donned, and sit around in our woolen undershirts once more. Was there ever a place of so many changes from one extreme to another?

Late that afternoon the tiny outlines of our comrades came into view, toiling down the ice. Knowing that the first thing they would say on reaching camp would be, "When do we eat," we promptly started getting supper. While waiting for the "hoosh" to cook, we took keen delight in watching the descent through field glasses. Mike, who was very much at home on skis, came flying down that terrific slide like the wind, skimming expertly over the rough surface. But the rest were not so expert and they came down the best they could. To put it mildly, they were not exactly graceful. Every now and then a ski would be caught in the snow, and over the wearer would go, rolling down a ways before he could regain his feet.

Norm and I had a lot of fun kidding them at supper, but Larry soon stopped that by telling us that the next day Mike, Norm and I would go up and find out if there was good prospect of climbing Nansen. "You're good little kidders, all right. Now we'll see how good you guys are on that hill." The tables had been turned!

And so we started next morning, December ninth. The ascent was hard work. It proved too steep and slippery to climb directly ahead. Step by step, moving sideways like crabs, we worked our way to the top of the ice fall. From there the route led up a steady slope, over crevasses, around boulders, up and over smaller ice falls. Finally we were brought to an abrupt halt.

At our very feet was a sheer drop of nearly two thousand feet. A man climbing up there in fog might easily have stepped right out into space and have whirled down, to lie broken at the base of that abyss.

Before us, spread out in majesty, lay the main Heiberg Glacier, pouring down through the mountain range. Blue and white, shimmering in the sun like rugged masses of cut-glass, it was a thing so wild, so full of barbaric beauty that we remained motionless for some time, looking down in awe and finding no words to express the splendor we gazed upon. It seemed like being at the very top of the world, and certainly we had done pretty well, for our barometer told us that we had reached an elevation of seventy-three hundred feet.

Our mission for this day was over, since evidently the back of Mt. Nansen was so steep and icy that weeks would have been required in order to reach its summit. An expedition would have to concentrate on it for an entire summer to do that job at all thoroughly. With all the other work planned for us we would not have time to negotiate this difficult bit of exploring.

The rest of the party had the laugh on us this day. Mike, as usual, shot downward as though on wings. But something must have been wrong with Norm and me. We certainly had no wings. At any rate, none that were in working order. We didn't even have our usual ability to keep upright on skis. I would take a header, and then, while Norm was laughing at my clumsiness, over he would topple. And if anyone thinks it is easy to right himself with seven foot skis on his feet, and a hummocky, slanting ice sheet for a floor—well, he'd better try it, that's all!

We finally made camp by crouching on our skis and sliding down, helter-skelter. After the fellows had finished razzing us during supper, we made our report to Larry. Realizing what we were up against, he decided our best plan would be to go to the other side of the basin for a day or two of exploration, and then return to Strom Camp, reload, and go further southeast along the mountain range. But before leaving we solemnly named this camp in honor of Martin Ronne, our sailmaker, who had also tailored our wind-proof boots and parkas.

A long, gentle slope was before us as we started out next morning and one by one the boys took off for a nice slide, their dogs racing along and having a lot of fun. Crockett and I were the last to leave, holding our dogs until the other got clear. Then, at a sharp command, our dogs leaped forward. It should have made a fine start, but as it happened, the gang line parted at the sledge and away raced the dogs, Fred and I after them, and the sledge was left standing alone on the hill.

And try to stop those dogs! They had been given an order to go, and they *went*. None of their business if the gang line broke. It took us quite a run before we could persuade those animals to stop, and then it was the leaders that halted and the others piled up on top of them. And maybe they didn't try to get into a glorious free-for-all right then and there! It took Fred and me about half an hour stopping fights and rearranging harnesses before we could lead them back up the slope and make another attempt. This time we got away with a good start, though the dogs took the whole downward rush as a frolic and we had to hold hard on the sledge to keep it from crashing down on top of them.

In climbing the glaciers and on other steep slopes we had rough-locked the sledges by looping rope around the sledge runners on both sides, and this rope dragged under the runners and served most effectually as a brake. Without this braking the sledges would have been banging down upon the dogs continually. As it was, we went a zigzag path wherever possible, as this was easier both in ascending and descending. But too often we had to take any path we could get through, with great bottomless gashes forcing us to beware. Perhaps the hardest of all would be when we would find ourselves walking along an ice shelf, while below us our path was paralleled by a deep crevasse. From second to second we could not be sure that either we or our dogs might not slip and be hurled down into that black, yawning mouth that seemed to grin up at us.

Two more days were spent in this basin, taking observations and getting rock samples. At the end of that time we returned to our base, carrying any number of small canvas bags filled with rock specimens, to be studied later on back in Little America. Larry was well satisfied with results and said that our trip up around Axel Heiberg and the foot of Nansen was, in itself, payment for the whole expedition. Although he had found no fossils, he had discovered beacon sandstone and that stratification had told him much of the geological history of the region. Then, too, the coaly material found by our party seemed to prove that the coal fields supposed to underlie much of the Antarctic land, went farther south than it has heretofore been possible for men to prove.

On the way back toward Strom Camp several of us climbed what we took to be Mt. Betty, hoping both to get a view of the eastern part of Axel Heiberg and, if luck were with us, find the cache that Amundsen said he left on that low mountain as he returned from his discovery of the South Pole. But there wasn't much of a view of the glacier to be had, and we found no trace of the cache. Disappointed, we made our way back to our camp and there made ready for the trip which was to take us along the base of the mountains and into that unknown area to the east.

It was on the thirteenth of December that we headed southeast. The trail led along close to the base of the mountains on a sort of shelf that jutted out high above the barrier ice. Seventeen miles were covered that day before making camp at the mouth of Axel Heiberg. How strange it was to look down on the barrier and see it enveloped in a milky-white sea of fog, while up where we were the weather was clear and fairly warm.

That night it started to snow. Big soft flakes drifting gently down "as though the angels were molting," Larry described it. All night that soft snow continued falling and all the next day and the next. It was impossible to move from our camp. Visibility was very bad, for the air seemed a milky-white and everything else was white, too, with no outline whatever. To wander ten feet from camp was to be lost.

Sixteen inches of snow fell, in all, but it was so warm that it melted when it touched anything and we were more chilled and miserable than when we faced a good cold, dry atmosphere.

Those three days we spent in sleeping and playing hearts, our favorite card game. Small squares of chocolate were the stakes and games were hotly contested. Then cigarettes started to get low and the few remaining to us made a real prize to contend for. Meantime the dogs spent a joyous holiday. Almost buried in the snow, they slept for hours on end, and despite the fact that it was a wet, clinging snow, instead of the dry, almost sandy sort we had had before, they certainly enjoyed the rest. Their heavy coats seemed to shed the wet.

One thing kept us from feeling cut off from the world, and that was our radio. Every second day, at longest, Fred contacted camp and one of the regular radio operators, either Hansen, Mason, or Petersen, would answer. Then, official business completed, one of the amateurs at radio, such as Dean Smith, would try his hand, and we would get the gossip of the past day or two. The routine would go something like this. Freddie would get his set in order and one of us would work the hand generator for him. Off he would click the call number and, as soon as he was answered, would report our position, the progress—or lack of progress—for the day past and ask for any instructions. This routine over, the amateur would come on and Fred would ask, "What you guys doing down there, any way?"

"Aw, nothin' much," would come back Dean's reply. "Just sitting and waiting for the fleet to come down from New Zealand and pick us up."

"Huh, can't you babies do something besides keeping the chairs warm while you wait for the *City of New York* to break through the ice? Why don't you get out and do some exploring before you go home, like we are doing?"

Somewhat nettled, Dean would flash back, "Why don't you get off the sledges and give your dogs a rest?" Then, relenting, he would give us all the latest news of camp and tell who was the big winner in the previous night's card game when cigarettes were the stakes fought for. We would hear about the midwinter sports and the latest political news that had been sent them from the United States, or the musical program and messages from friends radioed to them by special relay. Or he might say, "Ronne and Balchen want to know how your ski boots are holding out?" and express satisfaction at our reports on their wearing qualities and comfort.

"And how are the dogs? Dinty up to any new tricks? Pups keeping up their good record?"

Then Crockett would tell the latest performances of the dogs, and how the pups, that had always lived on snow and ice surfaces, did not know what to make of big rocks that grew warm under the sun's direct rays. But when Dean would begin to tell in great detail about the splendid dinner that George Tennant, the camp cook, had served them that noon, Freddie would immediately begin signing Dean off. Dean was only trying to tease a little bit, but to men who had been on scant travel rations for over a month, hearing about real fresh food wasn't as funny as it sounds. We could stand the monotony and lack of fresh foods without complaint, but having to hear an account of a meal of real meat and green vegetables was just more than we felt we had to bear. Still, at that, we certainly enjoyed being able to talk to the fellows every day or two. More than ever we appreciated the heroism of Scott and Amundsen and those others who had had to cut off all chance to communicate with the outside world when they hit the long, cold trail for the Pole.

It would have been a serious loss if anything had gone wrong with our radio. Still, before leaving Little America we had provided for just such an emergency. In our supplies we carried three strips of orange colored cloth and we had made a code that could be read by a plane passing over us. Thus, if the base camp had not heard from us for some days and had sent a plane to search for us, they would have followed to the last location we had given and looked about from there. If they had found the strips laid like a letter Z they would have known that we needed no assistance and wanted to go ahead, although we were unable to locate the trouble with our radio. If they had found two strips used to make a letter *V* they would have read this to mean, "Dogs giving out—may be unable to continue."

Another signal was like the letter *N*. This meant, "Dog food unsatisfactory—must have supply of seal meat to continue." A letter *H* would read, "Received your message and will proceed accordingly," while a triangle stood for "Cannot find message—please repeat." Had the three strips been laid parallel on the ice, those in the plane would have known that we were short of man food; two parallel strips would have signaled for dog food, and a single strip would have called for immediate emergency assistance, in case of illness or accident.

There was a whole series of these signals, and the men in base camp had a copy of them. They also had signals for us in case they could not drop a parachute with instructions. If the plane swung around and made a small *S* we would know they understood our signals. If it circled more than once we would be expected to give further information, but if visibility was so poor they could not see our signals, or we could not see them, they would jazz their motor as signal for us to set off a smoke bomb to assist them in locating us.

Fortunately we never had to make use of this code, for the radio behaved itself to the end of the trip, but when we remember how Scott and Amundsen and those other early explorers had to cut themselves off completely from the outside world, it is easy to appreciate what a help both aviation and radio are in aiding the explorers of today to keep in touch with the outside world. And, at that, there was quite enough of danger and loneliness and discomfort to satisfy the hardiest adventurer.

We realized that when the storm was over we would have pretty hard going, what with the wet, clinging snow and the badly crevassed surface directly ahead of us. Still, we were anxious to be off. Sitting around and playing cards is better than doing nothing, but we were six pretty well bored men at the end of three days. All the things we wanted to do in this new land, and here we sat —playing hearts! We felt we could get along for the rest of our lives without ever seeing a card again if only that snow would stop and let us make a start! Just think of all that undiscovered country all about us and the fact that we had food and fuel for a limited time; yet having to sit still and let the days go by. It was one of the hardest things we endured on all the trip.

CHAPTER XIII

INTO MARIE BYRD LAND

O N the seventeenth we broke camp. The snow had stopped and we could again find our way; so our march continued. It wasn't so bad that day, but the eighteenth is noted in my diary as most trying. Despite the snows that had hindered us for days, there was absolutely no snow along this part of the trail, nothing but solid blue ice, heavily crevassed. The dogs would speed up, the sledges would slew around, overturn, tumble into the crevasses, with ourselves following on several occasions. Luckily nobody was seriously hurt, and as we men were roped together there was no great danger—unless jagged ice edges should cut the rope!

But it was grueling work for men and dogs. The sledges took a terrific battering, the runners of one being completely torn off, and Norm's so badly worn down that we had to abandon it. Maybe we weren't glad to make camp that night! But, although all of us were completely exhausted, after a refreshing supper, all the fellows except Freddie and I were off to climb one of the lower peaks near-by and see what the surrounding country looked like. Freddie had a radio schedule to keep; so I stayed with him to furnish the man-power needed to crank his hand-generator. It certainly was fun, gossiping with the fellows in base camp, but we never got over the wonder of being able to make a few dots and dashes on the key and then be answered from four hundred miles away in less time than it takes to write about it.

This place was our furthest south, but the fellows came back with lichens they had found even this near the Pole. Larry was greatly interested here, for he found the mountains composed of some of the very oldest sorts of rock known. In fact, we all were interested, as Larry had taught us what he could about the different rock strata, though there wasn't much time for any more than a few general directions.

From this place we headed eastward. On the nineteenth we had to move out from the shadow of the mountains, trying to avoid the smooth ice, but it was no use. There just wasn't anything but ice, with here and there great bridged crevasses, and we finally had to take off our skis and cling to the sledges. The dogs went in a zigzag path and while they managed to get across pretty well, they often changed direction too soon and swung their sledges over the edge. Then there was work to haul them out and get going again.

Here the mountains were lower, seldom over five thousand feet, while those we had first visited were a full ten thousand feet higher. We were going down hill, too, and that made our progress faster, so that next day we made twenty-five miles. One trouble along here was to find a place we could camp. We had to have snow in order to stake down our tent, but for miles we would travel over clear ice, and mighty glad when we found a big enough patch of snow to provide a camp site.

On December 20th came a red-letter day, for we crossed the 150th meridian of longitude and entered Marie Byrd Land, first men ever to set foot on that part of the barrier. Think of it! Here was a part of the world no man had ever trod before! It certainly gave us a mighty thrill.

It was here that we were able to correct a mistake on former maps of the region. Amundsen, viewing the district from a distance had marked it as part of Carmen Land and noted an "appearance of mountains." Seasoned explorer that he was, he refused to assert definitely that these mountains really existed unless he could get close enough to prove that they were there.

Well, when we went trudging along where those mountains should have been, not only were there no mountains—there was no land! We were on level barrier ice and walked right through those non-existent mountains! Evidently Amundsen had seen a mirage. We had had experience enough with those things ourselves to know how easily a person's eyesight could fool him. Again we were impressed by Amundsen's wisdom in refusing to assert too surely a thing seen from a distance. When we returned to Little America we found that McKinley had photographed much of this district from the air on the polar flight. The camera confirmed our findings. Part of Carmen Land did not really exist!

We made camp on the mainland among the smaller bare mountains. On every side were glacial moraines of crumbled rocks that had been washed down by the slow-flowing ice during hundreds of years past. Larry was greatly interested and set to work studying the various sorts of stone and the surrounding land.

But first, as soon as camp had been established, we held a little ceremony on one of the foothills. An American flag was fastened to a short pole and this Larry planted on a little ice hill we had built, formally taking possession of the land for the United States. It was all most impressive and solemn as he said, "I here take possession of this land, discovered by Americans, in the name of Commander Richard Evelyn Byrd, as part of Marie Byrd Land, a dependency or possession of the United States of America." We had brought along our automatic camera and got pictures of this event, too.

Into the cairn Larry put a note citing the words he had used in claiming the land for America and stating that we were not only the first Americans, but also the first individuals of any nationality to set foot on American soil in the Antarctic. He listed the names of the Supporting Party that had helped make our trip possible and then listed our names. The date and latitude and longitude were given and the place named Camp Francis Dana Coman, in honor of our dietician and physician who had done so much to make our rations exactly what we needed in keeping up our strength and health. We also decided that a near-by mountain should be named Supporting Party Mountain.

But we hadn't much time for ceremonies. Soon we were all at work. Mike and I put in a day of surveying, while the others helped Larry with his geological inspection. Meantime the pups did a bit of investigating on their own that afforded us no end of amusement. Remember how a young dog, born in spring or summer, is puzzled by his first snowfall? Doesn't know what to make of the soft, melting stuff? Well, it was just the opposite with Sky and Al and the other youngsters. They didn't know what to make of the moraines and were constantly trying to chew up the small stones. Born on the barrier and driven only over snow-covered wastes, this was the first time they had ever camped on bare land. It took them days to get the idea that small stones couldn't be chewed or melted in their mouths. An illustrator would have had the time of his life sketching the puzzled surprise on the pups' faces when they tackled the moraine. Sky would lie down with a good sized rock between his paws and just growl at it, he was so disgusted. It was a wonder that there were no teeth broken during their experiments.

But we had put in all the time we dared here, for the season was getting late and our supplies were limited. The time had come to retrace our steps. Over three hundred pounds of various mineral specimens had been gathered and put in the little canvas bags for later study and distribution to various geological collections. Traces of copper and low-grade coaly material had been found, and various types of rock had been identified, but little metal was found. So far as we could see there was no trace of animal life in fossilized state, but a possibility of former vegetation was suggested by the finding of some lichens by Goodale, both on Mt. Nansen's sides and at our farthest south, 85° 27′.

It was in this moraine district that we used rocks instead of snow to hold down the apron on our tents. Also Fred Crockett and I began making bets as to how far Larry would go in a day. Along about the time we thought it would be a good idea to quit, we would begin yelling to each other that here was an ideal place to camp, with fine stones for weighting the apron. Or Fred might yell, "Bet you a cigarette that Simon Legree doesn't quit for another two miles," and I'd come back with, "Oh, I'll take you. He couldn't pass up a fine camping spot like that one just ahead of him."

Of course Larry knew what we were up to, but for all the sign he gave, our voices failed to carry through that still, clear air. No amount of teasing could make him abate a quarter mile of the stint he has set for the day unless he thought either we or the dogs needed to quit, or the weather turned against us. He would take any sort of risk except a needless one. That he rightly considered foolish to the point of being criminal, when so much depended on our success. But nobody could "kid" him into anything, and so our trying to tease him into making camp became a betting contest between Fred and me on the distance we would have to go, and sometimes ended by Larry throwing a ski pole at us or our finding his dog whip suddenly lashing about our legs.

I remember that one of those nights when we had made camp the talk turned on the geology of the district and Norm asked, "How come those mountains down here anyway?"

"Well, what do you think, Norm?" Larry queried, always interested in another's viewpoint.

"I'll bet it's a continuation of the chain that runs through New Zealand," Crockett put in. "At least that is my theory."

"You and your theories give me a big pain in the neck, young fellow," said Larry, but there was a twinkle in his eye. "What makes you think that?"

"Well—er—you see," and then, as usual we all laughed Freddie out of his theory for which he had no real basis; also, as usual. For one of our chief sources of amusement was listening to Freddie Crockett's theories. He had a theory on everything: on the best way to use skis, on dogs, on mountains, on snow, and anything else he happened to notice. Joking him about them and listening to Larry's pretended indignation at Freddie's contributions to science were part of the evening's fun. For Freddie, youngest of the party, had boundless enthusiasm and was given to hasty decisions on any and everything in sight. He would advance a theory but when Larry would ask on what his opinion was based, he usually had to come back with, "Well, I don't know. I just arrived at it, that's all." And then Larry would blow up.

But this night the talk went back to the subject of the mountains, and finally Larry said, "Well, it is far too early to make a definite statement, but it seems to me, judging from the little we have seen, that these mountains are part of a great fault block system that rises miles away to both the west and north. The flat sandstone structures that we saw checked with the ranges to the north that the British explored and it may be the same range. Although it was a popular belief that at one time this country was tropic, I don't believe there is anything really to substantiate that theory, at least in anything we have found."

It was that same night that Freddie used a phrase that always got Larry after him. Instead of asking directly for anything, with, "Have you some more 'hoosh'?" for instance, Fred would say, "You haven't any more 'hoosh', have you?" With that he would hold out his mug.

Larry looked at him coldly. "Yes, I have," he answered, making no move to fill Fred's mug.

"Well, how about having some?" Fred came back.

"You can have some just as soon as you learn how to ask for it correctly, you double-barreled idiot. This bringing up a youth is no job for an exploring expedition," Larry complained.

Fred came back meekly with "May I have some more 'hoosh', please, Larry?" and the lesson to the youth of our party being satisfactorily finished, we all grinned and settled down for some more "hoosh" and, when that was over, the inevitable cigarettes.

But travel wasn't funny these days. On the return trip to Strom camp the dogs suffered considerably from the heat. The poor things fairly stumbled along. Many times two or three panting beasts had to be unhitched and either carried on the sledges or allowed to lag behind until they were a bit rested and could catch up at the next stopping point. For their sakes travel was slower, and longer hours were allowed between hauls.

Our main work was done. Larry was satisfied that we had accomplished all that was possible in the time allowed us. A hundred and seventy-miles along the northern edge of the Queen Maud Range had been mapped and some knowledge gained of the geology of the region. Of course, more of this would be known when the specimens we had gathered could be brought home for careful study. Our immediate task had been to find all possible kinds of rock, and we had made a fair job of that.

We had found great glaciers in Marie Byrd Land, glaciers that came down from the mountains farther to the south, and while they were not as high as those further west, they were far more extensive, some of them extending as far as the eye could see.

Perhaps the saddest part of this return trip was Tickle, limping along with that torn shoulder muscle of his, falling behind and catching up hours after we had made camp. He was certainly the most courageous animal I have ever seen. Once or twice we wondered whether he could make the base camp. Norm even discussed with Mike the possibility of having to put him out of his misery, but neither one wanted that to happen if the dog could possibly get back to base camp where he could be taken care of and his shoulder given a chance to heal.

I remember one noon when we were through with lunch and ready to start, we could see old Tickle gamely coming into camp from a distance. We waited for him to catch up and then gave him a lift on one of the sledges; so he could have a rest. But soon we were in crevassed area again and Tickle had to get off and hobble along as best he might, for the sledges were going over the edge and he might have been hurled into the abyss below.

He seemed to understand the situation and followed along, sure that no matter when he got in, somebody would see that he had his supper, even if the other dogs had been bedded down hours before. And the other dogs did not quarrel with him, but let him settle where he pleased. Evidently they, too, admired his pluck.

CHAPTER XIV

A WHITE CHRISTMAS

TRAVELING slowly, saving our dogs all we could in the heat that was wearing down their strength, on Christmas day we reached a point five miles from Strom Camp. For several days we had been keeping a sharp lookout for some trace of Amundsen's trek to the Pole, for we knew he had passed through the region we were now traversing. But, so far, our quest had been without the slightest trace of the former trek.

This day we had made a fairly long distance and were glad to reach a convenient resting place near little Mt. Betty, lying slightly southeast of Axel Heiberg. Camp was made, and we were all wandering about before getting supper when Larry called out with more excitement than usually showed in his voice, "Say, fellows, look over this way. Doesn't that look like a cairn over there a bit to the northeast? Wouldn't it be great if it actually is the one Amundsen said that he left here near Mt. Betty on his way back from the Pole?"

We all gathered about Larry and peered off toward that dark speck in the distance. It certainly looked as if it might be a rock cairn over there. But we were too tired and hungry to try for it until we had had a hasty supper. Then Larry and Mike put on their skis and went over to investigate. Sure enough, there was the cairn that the first man to reach the South Pole had built on his return trip, over eighteen years before, and just about this time of year.

When Mike and Larry came skiing back and told us about it, we all felt that no better Christmas gift could possibly have been given us. Actually to see evidence of Amundsen's dash to the Pole! We were as excited as children. But we had had a hard day's pull; so decided to wait until after a good night's sleep before all going over to investigate.

Promptly after breakfast we put on our skis and went over to examine the cairn. There it stood, a carefully heaped-up pile of stones, some six feet in height, and on the inside were cached a five gallon tin of oil, a small piece of rope, some matches carefully wrapped from the dampness in a bit of oiled silk, and a note from Amundsen written in Norwegian, together with a list of the members of his party.

To be permitted to find and explore that cairn was

certainly a Christmas gift the like of which few men can match. To us it seemed the most wonderful imaginable. Everything was carefully examined, and then all the contents were carefully put back in place and the cairn closed. That is, everything except Amundsen's note went back. That we took to camp with us.

As soon as we reached our own camp, Freddie got his radio working and called the base camp. He told of our find, and then Petersen, the operator, sent for Bernt Balchen, who was also a Norwegian and could give us a translation of Amundsen's note. Then, letter by letter, Crockett spelled out the note in Morse code. The operator at Little America copied it as given, and he and Balchen, eagerly reading each word as it was written out, had sent back the translation to us in barely a quarter of an hour. The note told the date, what equipment the explorer had with him, the number of his dogs, that they were traveling fast on the way home, and general conditions. It read, as translated: *"Arrived and encircled the South Pole December 14-16, 1911. Have confirmed Victoria Land so that it is most likely that King Edward VII Land has no connection at 86 south latitude with Victoria Land. Also shows this land continues in a colossal mountain range to the south. Could see this enormous mountain range to 88 south latitude and most likely from its appearance it continues further in the same direction over the Antarctic Continent. Passed this cache on our return from the South Pole with provisions for sixty days, two sledges and eleven dogs. All are well. Roald Amundsen."*

While that was a most matter-of-fact little note, closing with a list of his party, to us those few plain lines in Norwegian told a tale of heroism and competent leadership that makes one of the romances of polar exploration.

We had decided to build a cairn of our own next to Amundsen's and leave a few more supplies there in case some other party might some day wander that way and be in need of equipment. Most of us had thought the cairn we found had contained most sensible material but Freddie Crockett didn't agree with the rest of us. Freddie, as it happens, has a healthy appetite. Without the slightest warning, at any time of the day or night, he could haul off and stow away a meal that would stagger two ordinary fellows. So when we opened Amundsen's cache and found nothing but oil, rope, and matches, Freddie took exception to the great explorer's consideration for those who had found his cairn.

"What! No food?" he cried. "Well, believe me, we won't let future generations down that way. You can't eat a lot of tin cans and matches. We'll build a cairn that will be worth finding. We'll give 'em some grub. Lots o' grub!"

And so it came about that when we went back next day and built our rock cairn next to Amundsen's, we put into it not only some extra clothing and a history of our party together with the tale of how we found Amundsen's cache, but also we put in some food, so that future explorers who have healthy appetites will not suffer the disappointment that Freddie Crockett did.

Will some other party some day find those two cairns? And will they have need of the oil and matches he left, and the food and clothing hidden beneath the pile of stones our group erected? Who knows? But one thing is certain. No party will ever feel a greater thrill than did ours when we realized that we six men, attached to the first expedition that ever flew over the South Pole, were handling relics of the man who first sighted the Pole and made his way there by hard, slow trekking over ice with dog teams. Our cairn finished, we retraced our steps to Strom Camp.

The time had come to turn back in earnest and make haste toward Little America. No telling when our ship, the *City of New York,* would come sailing into the Bay of Whales. There is but a short time each year during which the ice breaks up enough to permit a vessel to reach the barrier, and we knew that the Admiral was anxious to get us all out before the weather changed. Otherwise we might be frozen in for another antarctic winter of darkness and cold. Right after lunch on December 30th, our gear all repaired and the dogs rested, we began the long trek for home. Under graying skies we struck out due northwest from Strom Camp, thus avoiding the greater part of the glacial crevasses that had been crossed on our trip in.

With all extra equipment discarded, much of it in the cairn we had built near Mt. Betty, and relying for extra supplies on the caches that dotted our northern route, we should have been a gay party as we turned homeward. But somehow the fact that we were ending our adventure made us all a bit sad. As if to give us greater regrets, the mountains, that had been hidden and gray for days, suddenly appeared in a rosy glory of sunshine. There stood Mt. Nansen with his dark, rugged sides and shining top; the glaciers sparkled with all the colors of the rainbow, shimmering in their icy cataracts, and at our feet the barrier ice seemed a brilliant blue-green floor of glass with little white rugs of snow scattered here and there over its vast and shining surface.

No, it wasn't all joy, turning our backs on those great peaks. Still, there was pleasure in the thought of the physical comforts we would soon enjoy, and even more in anticipating comradeship with several dozen friends who were waiting for us at Little America. How we would enjoy hearing men shout and laugh and sometimes sing together. Just to wake up at night and hear the stoves being started, or the creak of snow under feet coming toward us! All the little sounds that tell one that other people are near had grown to be something for which we six all longed. And so it was with mingled feelings of joy and sorrow that we turned our faces southward and went flying along with our sledges. The dogs, after having a few days of rest, were as lively as ever, and we had to do some fast skiing in order to keep up the pace the teams set for us.

We covered twenty-two miles that day and then made camp. I doubt that any of us will ever again experience a New Year's eve such as that was. It had been miserably cold and foggy through most of that march and we kept going until late. It was about a quarter to

Strom Camp, named after Sverre Strom, who helped Bernt Balchen build the sledges, was used by us as a base of supplies. It was located close to the Axel Heiberg Glacier

A few minutes of rest seemed to revive the dogs, and after we had our "ob," they were ready again for the trail with perfectly amazing energy

twelve that night that Larry called a halt. We kicked off our skis and put on our furs. Then we got out the lunch box and sat down on the skis, our backs against the sledges, and waited quietly for 1930 to appear.

It was a strangely silent little group and the queerest-looking imaginable. Bitter winds and glaring sun had blackened us and scraggly beards hid us to the eyes. Our clothes were grimy and tattered. Larry had wound a long red scarf around his waist to keep his coat close to his body, and wore a blue stocking cap that stood up almost a foot above his head. This costume had lost him the hated name of "Simon," but he didn't seem to relish the new one of "Abdul" any better and usually chased us all over the place when we called him that, but tonight he was too weary even to protest.

None of us had anything to say. We just sat silent in the swirling chilly mist that at times was so dense that it made our clothing feel damp and left our cheeks wet. It was one of those dull, miserable nights, such as we have in a heavy spring fog at home. Thoughts of home, of years gone by, and years to come filled our minds. The high adventure of reaching the mountains was over and we had now ahead of us the hard trip back to camp. If ever we suffered the pangs of homesickness it was in those last moments of 1929 while we waited for the year to change.

Larry looked at his watch. Two minutes to twelve. He opened the food box, took out a thermos jug and poured us each a cup of hot tea. He then distributed Eskimo biscuit and a bar of chocolate to each.

Again Larry looked at his watch. Just twelve. "Happy New Year!" We shook hands all around. And thus ended the quietest meal I remember in the nearly two years we spent in the Antarctic.

But not all our experiences were heroic or serious. Life had its amusing side in this part of the world, as in any other. And nonsense seemed all the funnier against the background of real danger and adventure that marked our everyday routine.

One day while we were held up by fog on the southeast side of the crevasses, Mike and Fred grew mighty tired of loafing. So they decided to do some high-powered scientific work. They approached Larry with, "Let's get a sounding in this crack, Larry," indicating a crevasse about twenty yards from our camp. The crack was about a foot wide.

"We'll show you how a pair of real scientists should work, Simon," was Crockett's comment.

"And I'll show you how to break a couple of thick heads if you lose my sounding wire," came back Larry, grinning at them. "It's the only wire of that length I have and I want to take some depths myself when we get farther north. You may take this, but if you lose it, I am going to pitch you both in after it. Here it is," and he handed out his last long wire.

Accordingly, with much useless comment, those two daring fellows set to work. The rest of us offered some pertinent comments and then went on reading, comfortably settled on our sleeping bags in our tents.

It was peaceful in camp for about an hour. Then we

heard the two returning. They entered our tent and their guilty grins gave a hint of what we would hear.

"How did you make out?" asked Larry, without a quiver of an eyelash to show he had his suspicions.

"Well, not so well," answered Fred. "You see, something must have happened at the bottom of the crevasse. It must have closed or something because we can't get the line up. But it's all right," he added hastily, as Larry slowly rose. "We laid a ski stick across the top and tied the line to it. As soon as it gets free we can pull it up."

Larry dropped down again, mumbling, "Well, all I can say is that it had better loosen up."

Fred and Mike left our tent after a while and went over to the one that contained the radio gear. There was a lot of low conversation and moving about. Then we heard them leave camp again, this time going to the other side, nearer the crevassed area.

Another long, peaceful hour went by. Then again the crunch of snow. But this time they both went into the cook tent instead of the one where we were staying. A low murmur of conversation ensued. Then, "Hey, Larry!" It was Mike calling.

"What do you want?" Larry was interested in his reading. "I wish you two nuts would leave me alone."

"We know where there is a good sounding line."

"Where?"

"In the crack south of the tents. We can't get it up, though, and the ski pole is bent nearly double, it pulls so hard. Guess we'll have to wait awhile longer."

"And that ain't all," Fred chimes in. "There's another one on the other side of camp. But we can't get that up, either. But we will always know where there are two darned good sounding outfits."

Larry called them all the pet names he could think of, beginning with dumb, half-witted, no-good, flat-tires, and blamed idiots. Luckily we didn't have another chance to sound farther on as we had hoped to do. If we had, I am afraid Larry was mad enough to have lowered one of those two on a line. But that was one thing about Larry. He could get fighting mad, but he never lost control of himself and he never was mad at a *person*, though wild at something they *did*. Even when he was bawling out Mike and Fred, he couldn't help grinning at the fool stunt they had pulled.

It was while encamped on the barrier a little beyond the edge of the ice that we noticed an interesting phenomenon proving that the barrier is constantly in motion. All night long, at intervals of twenty to thirty seconds, a distinct hollow booming could be heard under our tent floor. At times we could feel the vibration of the whole barrier. The sound was very much like the slamming of a door in a large, empty house, echoing through vast spaces. It was Larry's theory that directly under us, jutting up from the sea, were mountain peaks that were part of a range extending from the mainland. The ice barrier, as it flowed over these peaks cracked and divided to keep on its course, and we, on the surface, felt the vibration of what was going on beneath us.

This is but a theory, yet it seems a logical one. High,

jagged peaks would explain the torn, twisted, distorted sector where the crevasses were so terrible, since the barrier ice would have difficulty flowing over such an area. The cause of the crevassed area may be a theory, but the noise on the southern part of the barrier was certainly a fact. The dogs noticed it, too, and for a time it made them restless. When a report was louder than usual, they would jump to their feet at the picket line and whimper. But gradually they grew accustomed to the sounds and only the worst reports disturbed them.

While most of the homeward path was over a route we had traveled before, that did not mean it was exactly as we had seen it on the outward journey. Here and there were new crevasses that had to be crossed or marched around for miles, if there happened to be no ice bridge over them. The weather was much foggier than it had been on the southward march, and we had a hard time making out the sledge ahead.

I remember one day there didn't seem to be any sky or ground. Everything was milky-white. Norm, skiing along beside his team a few hundred yards ahead, seemed to be walking on a white mist a few feet above the surface. My own dogs were just dark blotches, and I wasn't sure my own feet would touch ground at my next step. Looking back for a moment, I could see Ed Goodale coming along, but he, like Norm, seemed walking up in the air somewhere.

Then, just as I began to wonder if there was any hard surface or if we really were walking on clouds, didn't my leader go plunking through the crust of snow that covered the surface! In a moment the others were on top of him, unable to stop their pace in time. There was the usual result and when I got that bunch untangled and on the route again, there wasn't any question left in my mind about our being on a snow surface, though, unluckily, it wasn't any too solid. More than once my leader went through and had to be helped out that day. And always there was a pretty little fight to quell before they made their start again.

Chapter XV

BACK TO LITTLE AMERICA

NORTHWARD, over a marked trail, most of which we had traveled before, going was much easier. Supplies were waiting where we had cached them on the southward march. Perhaps it was easier than the outward trek, but the excitement of exploration was lacking. We were ragged and tired. Our dogs were weakened and suffering from the strain of the long trip as well as by the terrific heat of the direct rays of the sun. We weren't going to have these faithful friends of ours sicken and die now that the long, hazardous journey was drawing to an end.

Riding our sledges was no longer indulged in. Out on skis, we pulled with the dogs, helping and encouraging them as best we could. But something more drastic had to be done, that was evident. So, beginning just before the new year, we spent a day in camp and thereafter literally turned night into day. We laid up by day and did our traveling by night. This not only was cooler for the dogs, but it also gave us the sun at our backs and did away with a lot of eye-strain. The night sun moved along the horizon and sent long black shadows ahead of us.

Our day, or rather, our night marches were kept down to twenty miles or less. While the days were clear enough, nearly every night we met with severe fogs, but were able to pick up our marker flags without much difficulty. Although the flags were found, many of the smaller snow mounds had melted to a half or a quarter of their original height under the intense heat in the direct rays of the summer sun.

So we made our way back toward the base, and one early morning made camp near one of these snow heap markers. The dogs were picketed and fed as usual and we went to sleep as soon as supper was over. Everything was quiet and peaceful. If ever we should have gotten away to an uneventful start, that was the day. Imagine our horror, therefore, when we started to rout out the dogs that evening, to find a dark, purplish red dripping from the side of my snow-white Dingo, one of our strongest huskies! We had heard no fighting during the rest period, but here was the tell-tale stream.

I let out a yell and in a moment we all were gathered about the dog. The very ground where he had been lying was stained red. Norm and I were on our knees in an instant, but a quick search of the animal's hide revealed no wound. What is more, Dingo didn't seem to be in any pain, and let us handle him without a whimper or growl. And then, just as we began a fresh inspection of his pelt, Norm let out a loud and heartless laugh. He, who was usually the gentlest of us all with the dogs! We were all amazed, until——

"Look along to the marker, fellows! That dog isn't hurt. He's *dyed!*"

And so he was—dyed. Coming in tired and ready for sleep, we had failed to notice that the half-melted marker was one of those we had stained with analine dye. The dog had merely gone to sleep where some of this snow had run off, his body heat had melted it afresh, and the result was a dog that rivaled Gelett Burgess' famous "purple cow." The snows gradually washed away the color, but he was a gorgeous thing to behold for several days.

Poor old Tickle, Mike's leader, who had sprained his shoulder coming back on the eastern trip, had to trail behind. It was sad to see him come hobbling in just as we were getting ready to start every afternoon. Then he would take a big rest, and by the time we had finished supper he would pull into camp. As we could not carry him in the condition our other dogs were in, he had to do the best he could. But the brave old fellow kept this up all the way back to Little America. I sometimes wondered if Tickle didn't regard the little mishaps that held us up as special provisions to help him out. Several times, when we had trouble with the dogs or sledges, he would come hobbling up and sink down at one side with a little sigh of content and weariness. There he would lie, watching us get things to rights and start ahead, always with a few pats or words of encouragement for him, and then, after a little while, he would struggle to his feet again and hobble after us. We would glance back, seeing him grow smaller and smaller in the distance and wish we had some way to help him more. Good old Tickle. He had the courage that makes a real hero, man or dog.

And now came trouble with Norm's team. Dinty was a great dog and a wonderful leader. But slowly he began to show signs of what, in an opera singer, might have been called temperament. He wouldn't exert himself and sulked along in the traces, doing as little as possible and consuming as much time as he could in doing that little. Vaughan tried everything he could think of, petting the dog and encouraging him, examining him carefully to find if any illness or injury might be at the bottom of the animal's behavior. But, as far as anyone could discover, nothing ailed Dinty except a bad case of sulks. He was soldiering on the job.

Naturally, that couldn't go on without disorganizing the entire team. At last, in desperation, Vaughan retired Dinty to a rear position and brought the nine months old pup, Al Smith, up into the lead. He had had less experience than the others, but he was a willing dog, strong and eager, intelligent and easily taught.

And did Al Smith realize what had happened to him?

He most emphatically did! How his sensitive ears pricked forward and how his tail went up! You could almost hear him saying, "See me! Barely ten months old. And here I am leading our team. Maybe I won't show them all a thing or two about how a lead dog should act."

He certainly did show them. Without the older, more-experienced dog's ability to hold the trail, he frequently pulled off a bit to right or left when the snow was smooth. But, like all the others, he had learned that an orange flag or a colored pile of snow was the guide that ultimately led to food. No matter how far he had veered from the straight path, one glimpse at a bit of flying orange color, and Master Al turned sharply and made directly for the desired goal. Perhaps his charted course would have looked more like a series of two sides of a triangle than one good, straight line, but he got the dogs through on time, and his team was willing enough to follow where he led them.

As to Dinty, one could scarce imagine a sadder dog. The once proud waving plume of a tail was lowered, and the sparkling eyes looked duller. But the feet kept pace with his mates as the team pulled along. And so it went on, day after day, day after day, with Al proudly at the head, the shamed Dinty far in the rear.

When we got back on our old trail after the detour to avoid crevasses near the mountains, we were able to get our food supplies from the depots that we and the supporting party had established, and so were traveling light. But fog slowed us up considerably. It was on the fourth of January that there was a break in the mists near midnight and we had our farewell glimpse of the snow-peaked mountains far to the southward, shining out against a rose-tinted sky. Then the fog settled down again, but we were all grateful for that last view of a land we might never see again.

At last we were back at the crevassed area that had been so difficult to cross on the southbound trip. And here, of all places, a heavy fog caught us and we had to camp on the border a night and a day. The hot sun had been working on the surface and now the cracking of ice kept us awake. No sooner would we doze off from sheer exhaustion, than the horrible sound of a break, seemingly directly under our tents, would rouse us with a start. It certainly gave no sense of security to camp on a surface that was breaking into chasms all around us, while the fog made it impossible for us to move, or even to see what was going on.

Finally, after what seemed the longest twenty-four hours any of us had ever lived through, the fog lifted. Larry at once started out with a couple of us through the crevassed area. Before trusting the sledges there, he wanted to know what changes had taken place. Considerable action had completely changed our old trail, and it was evident that a new route would have to be followed. We went back, harnessed our dogs, and soon were under way. The new trail had been roughly marked, but it was hard going. Nor did it add to the sense of safety to have the continual cannon-like booming of breaking crevasses all around our path.

Once in a while, one of us would slip into a hidden crevasse, but the rope that held us bound together was the means of hauling the unfortunate one out again, sometimes a bit bruised, but otherwise unharmed. And then, coming down a long slope, racing along as the dogs loved to do on a down-grade, two of Norm's dogs started a fight. The other dogs in the team got mixed up in it and soon they were engaged in a hot free-for-all. Larry, a short distance behind, hurried forward, but his skis caught in a hidden obstruction, up he went into the air, and down he came like a thunderbolt in the midst of the fight. Those dogs had the life scared out of them! The fight was off. You never saw such a scared bunch of huskies.

Larry, unhurt, was lying on his back, yelling to Norm who was hurrying forward with the whip, "I'll show you how to stop fights, Norman. Throw that whip away. Ever see a fight stopped prettier than this?"

Meantime the other men had swung the gee-pole of their sledges way out in order to stop their teams from running into Norm's animals, and we all gathered round to laugh at the triumph with which Larry surveyed that group of scared, cowed dogs.

But there wasn't much fun going through that part of the journey. We thought we had learned all there was to know of the danger and discomfort during the past few days. And then, half way through that area, the fog caught us again. There was nothing for it but to stop. For all anybody could see, we might be driving headlong into a big crevasse. Even the dogs couldn't find their

way with surety in this fog. Terrible as it was, we had
to camp right in the middle of this region of horrors.

We managed to find a snowy spot where the tents
could be properly anchored, and then picketed the dogs
quite close by. The animals behaved well that night,
luckily, and we soon had them bedded down. When we
heard Tickle come limping in, hours afterwards, Norm
went out to give him his supper and an extra petting. He
found the others just beginning to be enough rested to
eat the food they had cached under their paws at meal
time. For once Tickle didn't have to eat by himself.

For two whole days we were held there, unable to
move more than a few feet from our tents, and then only
by feeling each step in advance. When we lay down
to sleep we were none too sure whether our beds were
on solid barrier or a thin bridge that might at any moment
crash through and land us in a bottomless pit. It was
on one of these days that we woke to find ourselves
camped between two deep crevasses. Ten feet to either
side in the fog and we would have met disaster. We
had to continue down parallel with them quite a way
to find a bridge we could cross.

We could sleep only in snatches, and even the dogs
were restless. On the second day, although it was still
foggy, Larry decided to risk getting out. The mist was
slightly less dense, and anything seemed better than
staying there any longer. We moved carefully as the
dogs were put back in harness and started off. They
did none of their usual mad dash to be off this day, but
seemed to understand the seriousness of our position.

It was slow, ticklish work picking our way through that torn area, but by going carefully and trusting much to the animals, we finally made it. Soon we were safe on the northern side of the barrier once more, with only one hundred and forty miles to go to "home." Looking back on those great pressure ridges and crevasses among which we had lived for days, the route ahead seemed easy enough to traverse.

For the remainder of the trip chill fogs were the only disagreeable thing to be faced. We started along smoothly and made camp one day with rejoicing that there were but ninety miles of travel ahead. While the rest of us made camp, Crockett, as usual, had put up his radio to get in communication with the base. Every day we had reported back to headquarters and received in return such news and necessary orders as they sent. But this night he came back with news that was quite startling. A message from the Admiral had just come through, stating that due to the heavy ice pack it was uncertain whether the expedition ships could reach the Bay of Whales this year or not.

To take all possible precautions against our being stranded another year, he was asking the captain of the whaling fleet lying beyond the Ross Sea to send their small chasers into the Bay of Whales to pick us up, if it was found that our ships could not get through. While awaiting a reply from them he suggested we cut our supplies and loads down to the actual minimum and try to reach camp in two days.

Two days! And we with ninety miles to go! That

would mean forty-five miles a day, more than twice what we had been able to cover of late. Fortunately he added not to put extra speed on until we heard from him the next night, as by then he expected to have definite news from the whalers. This message was sent in order to give us opportunity to plan ahead in case we were called on to make forced marches. While we appreciated being given warning of what might be required of us, it looked pretty bad for a while. In the event that anything should go wrong on the trail, a storm or fog descend, we might not be able to travel fast enough to cover the remaining ninety miles in time.

If the chasers arrived at Little America, we knew that they could not wait. They would have to pick up the men who were there and get out before the sea froze over. In other words, it looked as if we six men might have to stay in the Antarctic one more year. There was food enough and fuel enough at the base camp to take care of the entire expedition for another winter. We weren't worried about food, fuel, or clothing. Shelter was ample and we would probably have their radio to keep us in touch with the outer world. But none of us relished the idea of passing another night that was six months long, with a temperature of fifty degrees below zero.

There was another side to the matter of our getting back to Little America as quickly as possible. While we were anxious to make the ship, it was also true that we had some of the best dogs in the outfit with us. The sooner we could get back, the quicker these dogs might be given a rest and then be set to helping haul the goods

The sinewy bodies
of the trail dogs
were our guaran-
tee of safe return

Every driver had
a secret love for
the dogs of his
own team

*(Above) The trail party receiving a last word from Byrd,
November 4, 1929. (Left to right) Byrd, Thorne, Gould,
Crockett, Goodale, Vaughan, O'Brien*

*(Below) The return of the trail party, January 20, 1930,
after seventy-eight days in the field. (Left to right) Thorne,
Byrd, Gould, O'Brien, Vaughan and Goodale*

to be taken down for loading. Every bit of gear must be hauled by sledge from Little America to the ship, just as it had been hauled to camp when the ships were unloaded over a year before. Of course, many things would have to be left behind, especially if the loading was done in a great hurry, but there was some new material, like our geological specimens, that would have to be taken along. Altogether, the camp needed us and our dogs, almost as much as we needed them.

All night we moved ahead on the double-quick, that we might be that much nearer if the order to hurry came through. And all night we joshed each other, each trying to keep his worries to himself. Still, we all knew what the others were thinking, and at "ob," Mike let loose with a song he had composed to the tune of "Wait Till the Cows Come Home."

> *"Won't you wait till the dog teams come?*
> *Won't you wait till the dog teams come?*
> *Fir-po, Cy and Tickle, too,*
> *They all want to go with you.*
>
> *Won't you wait till the dog teams come?*
> *Won't you wait till the dog teams come?*
> *When Simon cracks his whip*
> *We all begin to skip.*
>
> *Won't you wait, wait, wait?*
> *Don't you pull your freight,*
> *Won't you wait till the dog teams come?"*

All pretense was gone when we made camp that night. Everybody pitched in and helped Fred get the radio up and then crowded round to get the news. And maybe we weren't a relieved lot when the Admiral told us not to worry, for our own ship would be able to come through and that that would give us ample time to make the base. Just the same, we sent Mike's song through to Little America, and for the next couple of days we were all humming it as we sloshed along.

But Mike and I changed our pace the next day, the same idea seemingly striking both of us at the same time. It was all because we had miscalculated the number of cigarettes that would be smoked on the trail. We had an idea that we wouldn't need more than about half the amount we used when loafing about in the dark of winter. But we got a surprise when we realized how many disappeared while waiting for supper or loafing a few minutes at the noon rest. So these past couple of weeks had seen us cherish the few remaining smokes. And suddenly Mike and I happened to remember a place on the trail where our abandoned snowmobile stood, and near it we had seen a discarded packet of cigarettes. On the way out that had not seemed worth picking up, but now—? Off the two teams started and there was a wild race, Mike and I both determined to secure the coveted prize of a few discarded cigarettes.

Neck and neck the two teams dashed, hurtling over the smaller ridges, dashing around the larger cracks, sometimes one leader nosing ahead, sometimes the other edging a length in advance. It was a wild race, dogs running as if their lives depended on it, men skiing for dear life and clinging tight as their sledges jerked over a rough hillock or dashed down into a rift.

At last! We wildly grabbed for the packet. I got it,

and Mike rounded his team up beside mine, certain that I would share some part of the prize with him. And then out of that promising-looking container I drew forth one lone cigarette, from which half the contents had filtered! Lucky we had some sense of humor left! We fumbled round until we found some cigarette papers and then solemnly contrived to divide the few dribbles of tobacco so that we each got two or three puffs.

On the morning of January 19, coming up a long hill about ten miles from Little America, we saw three figures hurrying toward us. They were Dr. Coman, Claire Alexander and Quin Blackburn, who were camped on a hill near-by doing a triangulation. Having seen us in the distance, they had dropped their work at once and hurried out to greet us.

Maybe it wasn't good to see them! They were glad to see us, too, though their remarks about our beards and complexions were not exactly complimentary. First greeting over, we were escorted back to their camp. Here Chris Braathan was waiting for us and had breakfast all ready to serve. Um! Maybe it didn't feel good to sit around and get waited on for once. We were all talking at the same time like a bunch of school girls, so great was the joy to meet friends again.

We rested there a few hours and then, after lunch, they escorted us to a new trail they had dug out. This was much shorter than the old route, having been laid out directly over the barrier, cutting off the bay entirely.

Before we started on that last pull, when we went to harness the dogs, Vaughan gave one look at the dispirited

Dinty and made a sudden change in his line-up. After all, Al Smith was just a saucy pup who would recover from any grief quickly enough. But shame Dinty by taking him back to camp in the line, and his spirit might be broken for good. He had been punished enough.

So when Vaughan began bringing out his dogs, he harnessed those next to the sledge first, then the next pair, and so on. Dinty, lying with his head on his paws and pretending indifference, was secretly watching the proceedings. When all the others had been put in harness and Vaughan went back to lead Dinty out to head the line and restore him to the lead for that last pull home, the big dog was fairly trembling with excitement.

Who says a dog doesn't think, doesn't understand, has no pride of position? They would have had their opinion reversed in short order if they could have seen Mr. Dinty step off on that journey. Head erect and sensitive ears pointing, his eyes fairly sparkling and that great black plume of a tail waving wildly erect, Dinty was again a lead dog to stir a driver's pride. His mouth open as he panted with excitement, the dog seemed fairly to smile at all the world.

And when Vaughan gave the signal to the animals, already tugging to be off, Dinty led the way as if he were not at the end of two and a half months' grueling work, but just out for a short run. So he brought the sledge back to camp, as he had led it out, as glorious a lead dog as ever guided his mates over snow bridges or swerved them expertly from a freshly opened crevasse which has suddenly yawned at their feet.

With the new route saving us a good many miles, the towers of camp loomed up about an hour and a half after we left the surveying party. The dogs smelled fresh meat and started to speed. A few moments later a great display of fireworks filled the sky. They were certainly giving us a great welcome!

We could see men moving about on the snow, some of them coming toward us. Then we dashed into a big pressure ridge and lost sight of camp for a moment. Out on the other side, we soon swept down to the base, and the whole camp was milling about, pounding our backs and pouring words of welcome on us. George Tennant, the cook, came hurrying out with big mugs of steaming coffee. And there was the Admiral, holding Larry by the hand and telling us all how glad he was to see us safely back, and that soon we would all, men and dogs, be on the way home to the States again.

But for this day, Little America was home enough for us. We had done sixteen hundred miles, much of it where man had never trod before, and come safely back, and were darned glad of it.

NOTES

THE following notes will serve to explain many of the text references where lack of space prevented a more complete description. They are taken from the actual reports, instructions, and data furnished the trail party in Little America.

PREPARATIONS

In preparing for the expedition, each man had certain special duties and certain supplies to look after. For these he alone was responsible.

A schedule read something like this:

Laurence Gould, in command. Also worked with Dr. Coman and J. S. O'Brien in providing the proper dog food, and man food.

Lists of supplies and weighing all materials on each sledge was the work of Gould, Vaughan, O'Brien.

Safety precautions and selection of bases: Gould and Vaughan.

Skis were selected and cared for by Vaughan.

Sledges, Dr. Gould, aided by Strom and Balchen.

Tents and dog harness, including whips and gang lines, were cared for by Goodale . . . Ronne helping with getting the tents satisfactory.

Ronne also made the food cases and sleigh sheets, but Crockett was responsible for seeing them made ready.

Navigation and flags were cared for by Gould and O'Brien.

Radio preparations were made by Gould and Petersen.

Arrangement of tents was supervised by Gould and Goodale.

Sleeping bags, Thorne, Crockett and Goodale managed.

All clothing except footgear and gloves, Vaughan looked after getting ready, while methods of keeping clothing dry were devised, after experimentation, by Thorne, Goodale, Vaughan, and Crockett.

Thorne and Vaughan looked after foot gear, while Goodale and Crockett saw to the gloves.

This meant not only seeing that the best possible articles were supplied but also weighing them and checking every item for every sledge, so that nothing was overlooked in packing.

MAN FOOD

The food ration for the trip was worked out according to recommendations made by Dr. Francis Dana Coman and represents a complete and well balanced diet.

Food Items	1 man 1 day	1 man 90 days	6 men 90 days
Pemmican	8.00 ozs.	45.00 lbs.	270.00 lbs.
Biscuits	10.00 ozs.	56.25 lbs.	337.50 lbs.
Butter	0.59 oz.	3.33 lbs.	20.00 lbs.
Peanut butter	0.29 oz.	1.64 lbs.	10.00 lbs.
Bacon	1.33 ozs.	7.50 lbs.	45.00 lbs.
Erbswurst soup	2.00 ozs.	11.25 lbs.	67.50 lbs.
Oatmeal	2.00 ozs.	11.25 lbs.	67.50 lbs.
Sugar	4.00 ozs.	22.50 lbs.	135.00 lbs.
Powdered milk	4.00 ozs.	22.50 lbs.	135.00 lbs.
Cocoa	0.14 oz.	0.83 lb.	5.00 lbs.
Malted milk	0.74 oz.	4.17 lbs.	25.00 lbs.
Tea	0.50 oz.	2.81 lbs.	17.00 lbs.
Salt	0.25 oz.	1.41 lbs.	8.50 lbs.
Chocolate	2.00 ozs.	11.25 lbs.	67.50 lbs.
TOTALS	35.84 ozs.	201.60 lbs.	1209.60 lbs.
Matches and toilet paper			12.00 lbs.

GRAND TOTAL 1221.60 lbs.

Little need be said about the above items. The pemmican is manufactured in Denmark and is the same brand so successfully used by Amundsen. The biscuits are so called "Eskimo" biscuits of Canadian manufacture and constitute within themselves a good ration. The other items with the exception of "erbswurst" are self-explanatory. Erbswurst is a highly concentrated pea meal sausage which has long been the standard ration for the German armies. It has further proved its great usefulness in the polar regions on other expeditions as well as on the Byrd Expedition.

DOG FOOD

The main ration of dog food is a dog pemmican compounded according to a formula developed by Dr. Malcolm, Professor of Dietetics at Otago University in Dunedin, New Zealand. It theoretically represents a correctly balanced diet. It had not been tried over long periods in the Antarctic, but on two short sledge journeys had worked out well. Innes Taylor, who has 13 expedition dogs sledging on Mt. Cook, New Zealand, used the same pemmican and in his report made this statement: "Dogs are in splendid shape and keeping that way on straight pemmican diet." Though he later questioned its use over long periods of time. However, the 1,600 mile sledge trip proved beyond a doubt that this pemmican was a splendid preparation for use over extended periods. The thirty-four miles covered on the last day of the trip is pretty good evidence of the condition the teams were in at the end of the long trek.

The geological party carried 2,674 pounds of this dog pemmican for use over the 90-day journey.

DOG EQUIPMENT

47 collar harnesses—this number allows 2 extra.
6 gang lines—this allows one complete spare.

 5 light steel-cable picket lines with chains for tethering the dogs when not in harness.

47 leash collars—this allows 2 extra collars.

 7 whips—1 for each driver, 1 spare and *1 for Simon*.
extra webbing, ropes, snaps and marlin for repairing harnesses and gang lines.

The certain loss of dogs accumulated all the further necessary equipment for replacements and repairs.

SLEDGES AND SLEDGE EQUIPMENT

 5 rigid double ended sledges of the Walden type used as lead sledges. Each of these fitted with two gee-poles—one on either side at the front.—2 canvas tanks or boxes to each sledge accommodated the supplies carried and thus obviated the necessity for sleigh sheets and an excessive amount of lash ropes.

 5 trailer sledges of Norwegian type which were of flexible construction. Two of these were double ended sledges which were entirely built by B. Balchen and S. Strom. The remaining three sledges were single ended Norwegian Army sledges which had been rebuilt and relashed by Balchen and Strom.
—each of these sledges was equipped with a single long canvas tank for these sledges carried the irregular articles more difficult to pack.

 2 sledge meters like those used by Amundsen. These were constructed to read in geographic miles and tenths of miles.

 3 man hauling harnesses. If more were ever needed they could easily have been made from the canvas and ropes in hand.

 1 extra wooden runner.

 3 bundles rawhide (100 feet).

COOKER

It has yet to be demonstrated that there is any more reliable or efficient type of burner for fuels in cold regions than the well known primus. The Cooker used by the Geological Party was built about a two burner Primus stove. It was designed and entirely constructed by Victor Czgeka after the principle which Nansen found so successful on his expeditions in the North

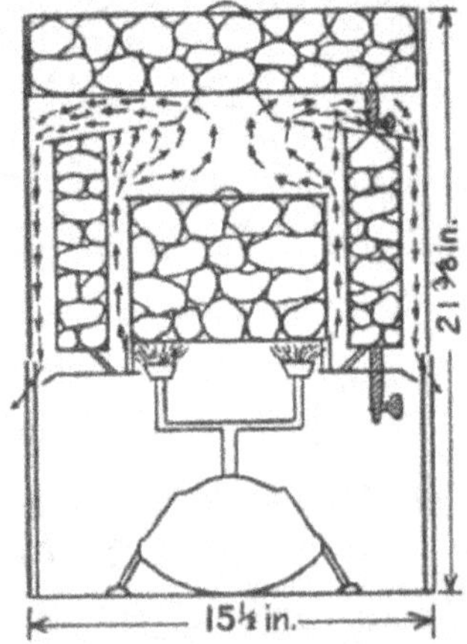

Nansen-Czgeka cooker so designed that capacity load gives water for entire meal—center pot furnishing the heated water, which, as needed, is replenished with the colder melted snow drawn from the ring and top pots, which have been utilizing any surplus heat.

Polar regions. It has therefore been designated the *Nansen-Czgeka* cooker. The diagrammatic sketch illustrates the construction of the stove and makes clear its method of operation.

FUEL

Experiments with various kinds of fuel were carried out in cooperation with Fuel Engineer Tom Mulroy. Petrol or commercial gasoline was found to be the best, both from the standpoint of calorific value and from ease of starting stove and getting it hot quickly. The *Nansen-Czgeka* cooker was tested in an atmospheric temperature of 30 degrees below zero, Fahrenheit.

The snow in the center pot was melted at the end of seven minutes and began to boil at the end of twelve. This represented about a third of a pot of water. However by the time the water in this pot had gotten hot enough water had accumulated in the ring and top pots to tbe drained off through the spigots and used for filling to center pot. By the time soup has been cooked in this pot a further amount of water sufficient for making tea had accumulated in the ring and top pots. The soup pot can then be removed, and a second pot, into which the water from the other two pots has been drained, can be put in its place. If the soup course is consumed after the manner of polite society a pot of boiling water for tea will be ready in the center pot at its end—and thus we have the complete meal in from 30 to 45 minutes—depending on how long it is desired to boil the soup.

TIME SCHEDULE

The following time schedule was worked out with an allowance of 20 per cent as a safety factor for bad weather and other unavoidable delays. Under similar circumstances Amundsen allowed 18 per cent as a safety factory and in spite of much bad weather found this to be much more than he needed. And it proved satisfactory for the Byrd Geological party.

The time intervals given in the table indicate the allowance for traveling from Little America to Depot Number 1 or vice versa, or from depot to depot as the case may be.

	Southward	*Distance*	*Northward*
Depot No. 1	3.5 days	44 miles	1.5 days
Depot No. 2	3.5 days	49 miles	1.5 days
Depot No. 3	3.5 days	50 miles	2.0 days
Depot No. 4	3.5 days	45 miles	2.0 days
Depot No. 5	3.5 days	50 miles	10.0 days
Depot No. 6	3.5 days	50 miles	2.0 days
Depot No. 7	3.5 days	50 miles	2.0 days
Depot No. 8	3.5 days	45 miles	2.0 days
Totals	28.0 days	383 miles	23.0 days

Stand by for flight........ 7.0 days
For geological exploration. . 32.0 days
Return journay ....23.0 days
                        ——
        Total.............. 90.0 days provided for

SUPPLY DEPOTS

While the text speaks of the depots as being fifty miles apart, this was a rough estimate. The actual distances were:

        Depot No. 1   44 miles from Little America
        Depot No. 2   93   "   "   "   "
        Depot No. 3 143   "   "   "   "
        Depot No. 4 188   "   "   "   "

These four were established by the Supporting Party, the Geological Party hauling part of their extra supplies to Depot No. 2, in order to lighten the load for the dogs as much as possible. At Depot No. 2 the Geological Party picked up their extra loads and established further depots:

        Depot No. 5 238 miles from Little America
        Depot No. 6 288   "   "   "   "
        Depot No. 7 338   "   "   "   "
        Depot No. 8 383   "   "   "   "

On the return trip the sledges traveled light, relying on getting supplies from these caches. Supplies were nearly 20 per cent in excess of actual needs, making allowance for delays in waiting for the Polar flight and being held up by fog and storm. Besides, if the plane had met with accident there would have been need for food to care for the men rescued from the airplane, so the supplies in the depots had to be calculated to serve in all emergencies.

The expected consumption of man and dog food on the journey southward, together with reserves cached for return are as follows:

To depot	Dog food consumption	Dog food cached	Man food consumption	Man food cached
No. 1	236 lbs.	45 lbs.	47.04 lbs.	100 lbs.
No. 2	236 lbs.	45 lbs.	47.04 lbs.	50 lbs.
No. 3	236 lbs.	63 lbs.	47.04 lbs.	100 lbs.
No. 4	236 lbs.	63 lbs.	47.04 lbs.	....
No. 5	236 lbs.	315 lbs.	47.04 lbs.	189 lbs.
No. 6	210 lbs.	63 lbs.	47.04 lbs.	40 lbs.
No. 7	210 lbs.	63 lbs.	47.04 lbs.	40 lbs.
No. 8	210 lbs.	63 lbs.	47.04 lbs.	40 lbs.
Totals	1810 lbs.	720 lbs.	367.32 lbs.	559 lbs.

The above data, together with the prospective amounts to be used in further field work can be summarized as follows:

MAN FOOD

Consumption on journey southward.........	376.32 lbs.	28 days
Stand by for Polar Flights.................	94.08 lbs.	7 days
Geological Exploration	430.10 lbs.	32 days
Return and Side Trip......................	559.00 lbs.	23 days
Totals	1459.60 lbs.	90 days
Man food cached last year............	250.00 lbs.	
Totals	1459.60 lbs.	90 days
Total carried by Geological Party..........	1209.60 lbs.	
Difference	250.00 lbs.	

In connection with the above figures it should be pointed out that 1209.6 pounds is a complete supply for 90 days—the extra 250 pounds consisted entirely of supplies laid the year before. This constituted a very generous reserve and emergency supply where it would be most likely to be needed—near the end of the homeward trip.

It is apparent from the foregoing time schedules that in case of emergency, in connection with flights to the south of Little America, the Geological Party will have at its disposal upon the time of its arrival 39 days of both man and dog food. This could be completely utilized without drawing upon the reserves planned for the homeward journey.

The foregoing preparations and plans were worked out upon the assumption that the field parties would have radio communication with Little America and with the planes. In the event that direct communication with Little America was impossible the following set of messages were to be used—the symbols being made from the three strips of orange cloth.

MEANINGS OF SYMBOLS ILLUSTRATED ON THE OPPOSITE PAGE

1. Good field—land in neighborhood of T and in direction which it points.

2. Fair field—landing should be all right if done carefully. Put skis down as close as possible to T.

3. Dangerous to land—unsuitable except in case of great emergency.

4. Impossible to land.

5. Wait for further signals—as for instance putting out T in some place a little distance from where signalling is being done.

6. We do not need assistance—unable to locate radio trouble. Anxious to continue.

7. Radio damaged beyond repair but everything else O. K. anxious to continue.

8. Shall we proceed according to pre-arranged plans?

9. Dogs giving out—may be unable to continue.

10. Forced to discontinue on account of dogs.

11. Forced to discontinue on account of men.

12. Dog food unsatisfactory—must have supply of seal meat.

13. Received your message and will proceed accordingly.

14. Cannot find message—please repeat.

15. Unable to carry out your instructions.

16. We need man food.

17. We need dog food.

18. We need immediate assistance—emergency.

19. We need fuel.

20. Would like you to land if possible without interferring with your plans. Desire conference with Commander.

. . . . It was, of course, assumed that field parties would be able to receive messages from planes by message parachutes. Plane would signal "understand" by making small "*s*"—indicate intention to land by figure "8"—desire further information by signals by circling more than once. A dip and on with plane meant everything O. K. Jazzing motor in near vicinity meant poor visibility from plane and desire to have bombs set off by ground party to assist in landing.

Orange cloth symbols as explained on page 190.

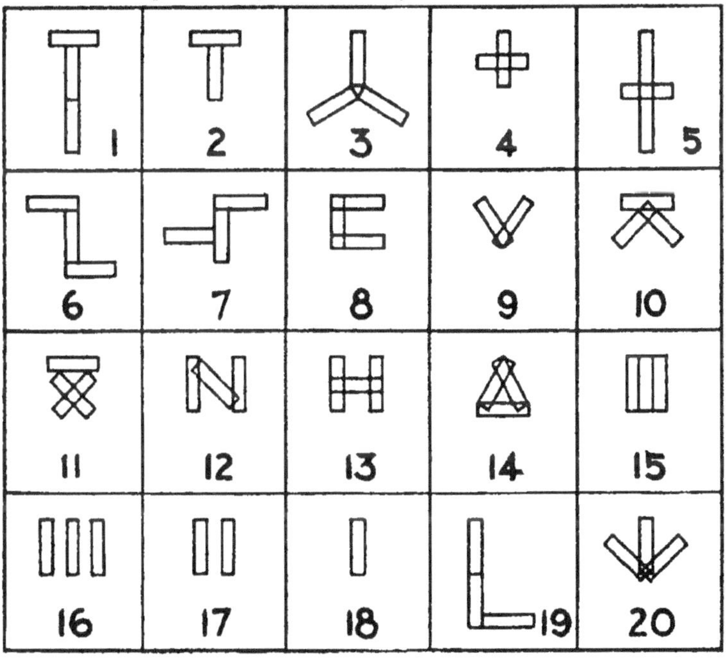

NOTE ON BYRD EXPOSITION DOGS

Thirty-five of the dogs came home to the United States. It was at first intended to leave them in New Zealand for use of future antarctic explorers, but there was fear that some of the animals might break loose and start a colony of wild dogs. Therefore they were brought back all the way to America, where most of them are now living on a Massachusetts farm. Very popular they are, and earn a small income for themselves by being exhibited to the many visitors who crowd to see them. A few of the dogs are still with their owners, Dinty being still with Norman Vaughan and Al Smith in the possession of Laurence Gould.

SOUTH · POLE
AMUNDSEN DEC. 14. 1911
SCOTT JAN. 18. 1912
BYRD NOV. 29. 1929
Queen Maud Range
Amundsen's Cairn
Crevassed Area
N

Pressure Ridges
Ross
W

www.ingramcontent.com/pod-product-compliance
Lightning Source LLC
Chambersburg PA
CBHW050334160726
48002CB00001B/310